WASHINGTON
vs.
MAIN STREET
The struggle between
federal and local power

WASHINGTON vs. MAIN STREET

The struggle between federal and local power

by JULES ARCHER

ILLUSTRATED WITH PHOTOGRAPHS

THOMAS Y. CROWELL COMPANY · NEW YORK

Designed by Carol Basen
Manufactured in the United States of America

Library of Congress Cataloging in Publication Data
Archer, Jules.   Washington vs. Main Street.
SUMMARY: Chronicles the struggles between Federal and local power from before the Declaration of Independence through the present.   Bibliography: p.   1. Federal government—United States—Juv. lit. [1. Federal government. 2. Local government] I. Title.   JK325.A77 353   74-8623 ISBN 0-690-00005-7

1   2   3   4   5   6   7   8   9   10

To our acquired daughters,
in their order of appearance,
Mary Fran Archer
Elizabeth Archer
Janet Catherine Archer
with great affection

• *Contents*

WASHINGTON
vs.
MAIN STREET
*The struggle between
federal and local power*

1 · Washington vs. Main Street

*D*oes *your local school board have the right to defy a* Federal court order to integrate schools by bussing students from your neighborhood school to one situated miles away?

If your family is forced on welfare because your mother is divorced or widowed and must stay home to look after the small children, does the town, county or state have the right to cut her off welfare rolls if she refuses to take a job?

Does your local school board have the right to compel students in your family to say a prayer or the Pledge of Allegiance each school day, if they object for any reason whatever?

If your state legislature decides that a war activity of the Federal government is illegal or unjust, do you have the right to refuse to be drafted for it?

Does your state legislature have the right to change your voting district, so that another district with only 500 people will have the same representation as yours with 5,000?

Do you have the right to expect that your area or state will get back a proportionate share of the Federal taxes paid by your family in grants for local benefits?

Does Washington guarantee your right to move into a neighborhood where the homeowners have agreed not to sell homes to citizens of your race or religious faith?

If yours is a farm family, do you have the right to expect a Federal subsidy to keep your farm in business?

Where do you look for help in holding down prices, preventing rent increases, and controlling electricity rates?

Do industries in your area have the right to pollute the air and water as long as the state legislature permits them to do so, because they provide necessary jobs and taxes?

If you are suspected of breaking the law, does a policeman or state trooper have the right to break into your home to search for evidence of the crime? To make you confess?

The answers to those and similar questions affect the lives of all of us, and are closely tied up with a struggle for power that has been waged between Washington and Main Street ever since the founding of our Republic.

Because the Constitution defines the areas of Federal and state authority only in general terms, politicians have persistently fought over the rights of each level of government. Conflicts have arisen between presidents and governors; between Congress and the President; between state legislatures and Congress; between the Supreme Court and state legislatures; between the cities and all other agencies of government. Who has the power to do what, in which areas, on what occasions?

Of crucial importance to all Americans are the limits of presidential power, which were so painfully called into question during the Watergate scandal of the Nixon administration. These limits are important to define since they affect a president's ability to take the country to war; to conceal mistakes and wrongdoing from the people; to misuse investigatory powers; and to violate the constitutional rights of citizens and local governments on grounds of "national security."

In this book the term "Washington" is used as shorthand for Federal forces, usually representing either the President, Congress or the Supreme Court, even though the three branches of national government are often in conflict with each other. The term "Main Street" represents government and voters at local levels—state, county, city, town, suburb and village.

Congress wears two hats in the struggle between Washington and Main Street. The average congressman is often torn between voting the demands of his home district or state and voting for what his conscience tells him is best for the nation. Should he, for example, vote to shut down a superfluous defense plant in his district to save American taxpayers money? Or should he vote to keep it open to save jobs for his constituents?

One 1965 survey found that 28 per cent of a congressman's time, and 41 per cent of the time of his staff, was devoted to servicing demands from back home, rather than to considering pending national legislation. In 1821 a Congress anxious to vote on a highly important bill was forced to twiddle its thumbs because Representative Felix Walker of North Carolina insisted upon making an endless speech on behalf of his constituents back home in Buncombe County. After pleas and groans failed to shut him up, Congress immortalized him by labeling all such windy political speeches "buncombe," today called simply "bunk."

Most historic decisions of the Supreme Court have come about as a result of cases fought over the interpretation of the Tenth Amendment. It declares, "The powers not delegated to the United States by the Constitution, nor prohibited by it to the States, are reserved to the States respectively, or to the people."

To this day political battles rage between those who want Federal power limited strictly to the exact letter of the Constitution and those who argue for "implied powers"—a broad interpretation of the Constitution—to permit the use of Federal power where it is not specifically denied to Washington.

The pendulum of American history has swung back and forth between presidents (supported by conservative "haves") who scaled down government spending and held Federal intervention to a minimum and presidents (supported by liberal "have-nots") who introduced far-reaching Federal legislation.

Our daily lives are lived largely under local, not Federal, control. Justice, most of the time, is administered for us in local, county or state courts. Most of our roads are planned, built and maintained locally. Police, health, welfare, education, safety, licensing, marriage, divorce, and birth and death processes are all areas under the control of the state and its local subdivisions.

Champions of Main Street insist that the states are separate sovereignties whose basic rights were not forfeited by the compact with other states in 1787 that led them to accept the Constitution. In that view, whenever Washington "exceeds its authority," dissident states can exercise the right of nullification or, if this is denied, secession.

Those who invoke states' rights generally hold a conservative viewpoint. They have raised this argument to deny civil rights to black Americans; to prevent the regulation of big business; to legalize child labor; to oppose the eighteen-year-old vote; to stop Federal dams and power projects; to curb freedom of speech; and to hamper union organizing.

Powerful private interests often seek a transfer of as much governmental power as possible from Washington to Main Street, because it is easier to lobby and manipulate local government than it is to restrict either the President or Congress.

In seeking to define the elusive boundaries between Federal and state power, the Supreme Court has often reversed its decisions when the ratio of liberal to conservative justices has changed. Such reversals have also been influenced by the appointment of a new Chief Justice, as well as by marked shifts in the national mood.

"What's the good of your Supreme Court?" asked one Australian observer. "It never seems to settle anything. No sooner does the Court decide against one state's attempt to violate a Federal law than another state breaks it again, using new arguments. Why does the Federal government have to fight the same issue all over again, all the way back up to the Supreme Court—which may then change its mind?"

The answer may well be that unless every citizen and state always has the right to challenge the constitutionality of any Federal law with fresh arguments, we would have a closed society, not a democracy capable of constructive change, as well as the protection of our rights and freedoms.

The fight between advocates of Federal and local power began even before the Declaration of Independence. Representatives at the Continental Congress were reluctant to transfer any authority from their colonial legislatures to a strong new Federal government, even for the sake of the Revolution. Mistreatment by the powerful British Empire had made them suspicious of accepting the yoke of any new central power.

The Articles of Confederation, which the Second Continental Congress agreed upon in November 1777, was the only loose plan of union they would have considered. It carefully stipulated, "Each State retains its sovereignty, freedom and independence, and every Power, Jurisdiction and right, which is not . . . expressly delegated to the United States."

The Confederation rested on the authority of the states, not directly on the people. Each state government acted independently, with little regard for the weak new nation it had joined. States delayed sending desperately needed money and troops to George Washington. Serious inflation hurt the war effort because each state printed its own paper money freely to finance its own operations.

Worried Federalists urged that Congress be given the power to assess and collect taxes, along with other powers designed to strengthen the central government. Suspicious Americans accused them of scheming to establish an aristocracy and destroy newly won liberties. John Jay wrote glumly to George Washington in June 1786, "To oppose popular prejudices . . . and expose the improprieties of States, is an unpleasant task, but it must be done."

The Federalists called a Constitutional Convention in Philadelphia in 1787 to draft plans for a new system. One issue almost wrecked the Convention—insistence by the larger states that voting in Congress should reflect population, instead of following the one-state, one-vote rule of the Articles of Confederation. The compromise that saved the day was the creation of a Senate, with equal state representation, and a House with proportional representation.

The final Constitution provided for power to be shared between the states and the Federal government, with a system of checks and balances to prevent any excess of power from being grasped by the President, Congress or the Supreme Court.

A hot debate broke out in the Virginia legislature over Article VI, which specified that acts of the Federal government were to be accepted as "the supreme law of the land," binding upon all states. "This power is calculated to annihilate totally the state government!" cried George Mason. Patrick Henry thundered, "Trial by jury, liberty of the press . . . all pretensions to human rights and privileges, are rendered insecure, if not lost, by this change."

He denounced the framers of the Constitution for presuming to speak in the name of "We, the people," since he saw the Constitution simply as a compact between state governments. In

Pennsylvania, James Wilson disagreed: "This is not a government founded upon a compact. It is founded upon the power of the people."

In 1793 the sovereignty of the state was tested by a suit of South Carolinians against Georgia for seizing property they owned in that state. Georgia challenged the Supreme Court's jurisdiction in the matter, and refused to send counsel to argue the case. A state could not be sued, Georgians insisted, without its consent. But the Court ordered Georgia to recognize the property rights of U.S. residents of other states (*Chisholm v. Georgia*). Enraged, the Georgia legislature passed a law making it a crime punishable by death for anyone to execute that order of the Supreme Court.

Virginia rallied to Georgia's defense, expressing fear of the Court for "invading states' rights." In 1794 Congress responded by passing the Eleventh Amendment, denying the Court the power to sit in judgment on suits against a state by citizens of another state or nation.

By the treaty that ended the Revolutionary War, however, the American government agreed to respect debts owed by Americans to British creditors. This provision conflicted with an earlier (1777) Virginia law declaring such debts null and void. The Supreme Court held in 1796 that Virginia debtors had to pay up, because under the Constitution national treaties represented the supreme law of the land, canceling out any conflicting state laws (*Ware v. Hylton*).

In 1801 President John Adams appointed his Secretary of State, John Marshall, Chief Justice of the Supreme Court. "My gift of John Marshall to the people of the United States," Adams said later, "was the proudest act of my life." It was Marshall whose decisions over the next thirty-five years made history by broadly interpreting the Constitution to establish Federal power as supreme, binding the states firmly together as one nation. Again and again he struck down state laws which conflicted with the Constitution and the laws of Congress.

Jefferson complained that the Constitution was but "wax in the hands of the Judiciary." When he became President, ironically, his Louisiana Purchase stretched the use of Federal power under the Constitution much further than any decision by Marshall. Nothing in the Constitution authorized a president to undertake such a gigantic real-estate transaction, nor to annex a foreign people into the Union.

Ironically, the Federalist New England states, which might have been expected to approve such vigorous Federalism, threatened to secede as a Northern Confederacy instead. They feared that the South and West would carve states out of the Louisiana Territory that would give them an agrarian and frontier balance of power over the industrial and commercial Northeast.

When the proposed state of Louisiana, the first carved out of the Purchase, sought admission to the Union, Representative Josiah Quincy of Massachusetts warned grimly, "If this bill passes . . . it will free the States from their moral obligation. . . . [Many will] prepare for separation . . . violently if they must."

Jefferson was still very much concerned with protecting states' rights—not now from Congress or the White House, however, but from the Supreme Court, which he viewed as an arm of Federalism.

As western immigration boomed, the South and North clashed over the right of Washington to limit western public land sales. The South insisted that such attempts were infringements on states' rights. Senator Robert Hayne of South Carolina, speaking for Vice President John C. Calhoun, insisted that the states must be allowed to decide when the Federal government was exceeding its constitutional powers and to nullify such acts. Otherwise, he told Congress, "the States are at once reduced to mere petty corporations, and the people are entirely at your mercy."

Daniel Webster of Massachusetts challenged, "I must now beg to ask, sir, whence is this supposed right of the states derived? Where do they find the power to interfere with the laws of the Union?" The Federal government, he insisted, "is not the creature of the State Governments." To states' righters who cried, "Liberty first and Union afterwards," Webster replied, "Liberty *and* Union, now and forever, one and inseparable!" Without supreme Federal authority, he demanded, "is not the whole Union a rope of sand?"

Yet in 1831 the doctrine of states' rights was so widely held that Alexis de Tocqueville, the young French nobleman who studied the American system firsthand, observed in his travels, "In America the legislature of the state is supreme; nothing can

BORN TO COMMAND.

OF VETO MEMORY.

HAD I BEEN CONSULTED

KING ANDREW THE FIRST.

President Jackson's assertion of Federal power inspired this contemporary cartoon, which portrayed "King Andrew" trampling on the Constitution and the "Judiciary of the U. States."

(CULVER PICTURES, INC.)

impede its authority. . . . Under its immediate control, is the representative of executive power."

Acting in this conviction after the Mexican War, Texas claimed part of newly won New Mexico, vowing to seize it if necessary. President Zachary Taylor angrily warned Texans, "If Texas militia march into any one of the other States or into any Territory of the United States, there to execute or enforce any law of Texas, they become at that moment trespassers." Faced with the prospect of fighting a Federal army Taylor was ready to send against them, the Texans backed down.

The Civil War, which will be discussed later, was of course the classic confrontation of Federal versus state power, ending—for a while at least—the challenge of states' righters.

The end of the Civil War saw the rapid growth of corporations which prospered by combining in trusts unchecked by Federal power for most of the second half of the nineteenth century. This trend was not seriously reversed until the Wilson administration in 1912, when reform legislation swept aside state laws favoring the corporations and broke up many monopolies.

The end of World War I, however, brought a dozen Republican years that restored "normalcy." Presidents Warren Harding, Calvin Coolidge and Herbert Hoover followed a hands-off-the-economy policy, letting state power once more take precedence over Federal power.

"The American system . . . is founded upon . . . self-government in which decentralized local responsibility is the very base," Hoover declared, adding, "When the Republican Party came into full power . . . it restored the Government to its position as an umpire instead of a player in the economic game." He urged Americans to embrace "rugged individualism," not Federalism.

As governor of New York (1928–1932), Franklin D. Roosevelt at first agreed, championing states' rights. But when the Depression crippled the United States, throwing fifteen million Americans out of work and plunging their families into destitution, he grew convinced that only the Federal government could provide relief, jobs and direction to get the country back on its feet.

At his inaugural in 1933, FDR told the nation that he would "ask the Congress for the one remaining instrument to meet the crisis—broad Executive power to wage a war against the emergency, as great as the power that would be given to me if we were in fact invaded by a foreign foe."

In the frenzied initial hundred days of the New Deal, he introduced major laws on banking, securities regulation, currency, production and price codes, control of agriculture, public works, unemployment relief, reforestation, public power, social security and taxation. Never before in American history had Federal power been used so sweepingly. Never before had an American president made the White House so supreme a force in governing every state in the land.

Republicans and conservative Democrats were appalled, fearful that Roosevelt was leading the country into socialism. Hoover urged that all regulatory powers over economic affairs be turned over to the states. "We must maintain . . . a sense of responsibility in the states," he insisted. "It is the local communities that can best safeguard our liberties."

But Roosevelt continued to use Federal power boldly, expanding it into every corner of the nation's life, and changing the lives of all Americans dramatically. His reelection to four terms indicated that the vast majority of citizens approved of having a strong president in the White House to look after their interests. Observing that most Americans believed in the let-George-do-it solution to the country's troubles, he grinned, "I began to think sometimes that my first name was George."

"He was in a very special sense the people's President," observed Supreme Court Justice William O. Douglas, "because he made them feel that with him in the White House they shared the Presidency. . . . [He] gave even the most humble citizen a lively sense of belonging."

FDR's vast use of Federal power brought him into conflict with a conservative Supreme Court. During his first administration, the "strict constructionist" Court threw out New Deal legislation as unconstitutional in case after case. Accusing it of belonging to the "horse-and-buggy age," Roosevelt angrily sought to add six new justices to the Court on the grounds that the "nine old men" were too decrepit to function properly. His plan to stack the Court failed, but his radio "Fireside Chats" aroused public opinion to demand that it uphold New Deal acts which replaced those it had struck down. Soon, too, older justices died or retired, and were replaced by Roosevelt appointees favorable to the President's "implied powers."

Running for a second term, he was once more denounced by Hoover for his "plans to invade States' rights, to centralize power in Washington. . . . Those ideas were born of American radicals." The Republican candidate in 1936, Alf Landon, told an Albuquerque audience, "Franklin D. Roosevelt proposes to destroy the right to elect your own representatives, to talk politics on street corners, to march in political parades, to attend the church of your own faith, to be tried by jury, and to own property." But Americans did not believe it. FDR was voted back to office by every state except Maine and Vermont.

By the time he died early in his fourth term, FDR had firmly established the paramount power of Washington over Main Street, emphasized by the exercise of sweeping war powers. Three years later, journalist John Gunther noted, "The 'sovereignty' of the states today is largely artificial; the old doctrine of states' rights has been pretty well rubbed down, and most states

. . . are little more than a superior type of county. The tremendous federal bureaucracy of the New Deal; such interstate conceptions as that expressed by TVA; incessant movements of population from one state to another . . . federal grants as for highways . . . these and a hundred similar items have tended to reduce . . . state authority."

President Harry S. Truman continued FDR's policy of a strong central government, winning the 1948 election despite a revolt of angry southern Democrats led by Senator Strom Thurmond into an opposition States Rights Party. Some northern states were irked, too. At the 1951 Governors' Conference Governor Val Peterson of Nebraska lamented, "We surrendered our control . . . the day we took the first dollar of Federal grants-in-aid."

Under Republican President Dwight D. Eisenhower, however, the balance of power was once more reversed, with the Federal role reduced and state governors elevated to important status, having a greater voice in Federal and state affairs. The one exception to this trend was the administration's reluctant enforcement of the surprise decision of the Supreme Court in *Brown v. Board of Education of Topeka* (1954), an historic ruling by Chief Justice Earl Warren requiring all states to integrate their public school systems. This decision touched off furious opposition by southern governors, notably George Wallace of Alabama and Orval Faubus of Arkansas.

The pendulum swung again from Main Street to Washington with the accession of John F. Kennedy to the White House in 1960. He declared, "There are those who say that we want to turn everything over to the Government. . . . The argument has been used against every piece of social legislation in the last twenty-five years. . . . I don't believe in big government, but I believe in effective government action, and I think . . . it's the only way that we're going to move ahead."

States' righters in the Congress, however, were able to block most of his New Frontier program. They were frustrated when, after Kennedy's assassination, Lyndon Johnson assumed the Presidency and successfully introduced a Great Society program involving a vast new exercise of Federal power.

Opposing Johnson in the 1964 elections, Senator Barry Goldwater of Arizona declared, "We Republicans define government's role . . . preferably through the one closest to the people involved; our towns and our cities, then our counties, then our states, then our regional contacts and only then the national government. That, let me remind you, is the land of liberty built by decentralized power. . . . Choose the way of this present Administration and you will have . . . the regimented society, with a number for every man, woman, and child, a pigeonhole for every problem, and a bureaucrat for every decision."

Johnson introduced legislation initiating sweeping national changes, especially for ethnic minorities, but its impact was dissipated by rising dissatisfaction over the Vietnam War and civil disturbances. An angry sense of powerlessness on Main Street gave Richard M. Nixon an opportunity to win the White House. In his bid for election in 1968, he developed a "Southern strategy" designed to win votes in the South, which had been traditionally Democratic since the Civil War.

Nixon called for "interpreting the old doctrine of states' rights in new ways"—a clear signal that he intended to use legal stratagems to sabotage the Supreme Court order on school integration. He promised a greater degree of local control and self-government by decentralizing Federal operations, allowing Main Street to make its own decisions.

Once elected, Nixon used his presidential powers sweepingly, expanding the war in Vietnam into Laos and Cambodia, and setting up an organization of secret political police to use against Democrats and antiwar demonstrators. These and other abuses of Federal power came to light in the Watergate scandal that rocked the nation in 1973 and threatened him with impeachment.

With American involvement in the Vietnam War largely behind him by 1973, the President began his second term by turning his attention to domestic matters. He told Americans that he intended to end the centralized power that had marked their government for the first seventy years of this century. It was inefficient, wasteful, unjust and character-crippling, he insisted, to encourage citizens to look to a Washington bureaucracy for solutions to all their problems.

Such problems, said the President, could be solved much more fairly, efficiently and thriftily at the local level—by people in town halls, city councils, county seats and state legislatures. He proposed decentralizing the operations of government and dividing them up among the states.

Washington would no longer spend and control the bulk of public funds, except for the military budget. Instead, a revenue-sharing program would give the states a large share of the money raised in Federal taxes, so that they could spend these funds on state, county, city and town programs as they saw best. Nixon also proposed to eliminate or consolidate major Federal agencies, and to end many Federal grants-in-aid programs.

"Mr. Nixon . . . seems set on remaking the basic balance of American government," observed *Newsweek*, "concentrating more power in the White House and proportionately less on Capitol Hill." It was not presidential power that he sought to weaken but congressional power, while he enhanced the powers of state governors. And he appointed four new justices to the Supreme Court whom he could count on for a "strict constructionist" view of the Constitution favoring states' rights.

When a CBS interviewer asked Nixon's chief aide for domestic affairs whether the President wasn't trying to effect one-man rule, John D. Ehrlichman replied, "Sure, that's what the President of the United States is for." The sensational disclosures that came out of the Senate Watergate hearings seemed to bear out this White House view of the presidency.

With this brief study of the struggle between Federal and state power throughout our history as background, it is time to examine how that struggle affected—and still affects—our lives in the schools we attend and the jobs we hold; our health; the civil liberties we enjoy; our national defense; our voting rights; the taxes we pay; our rights as minorities; the aid to our cities; our transportation; the homes we live in; help to farmers and labor; the things we buy; and the air, water and land we depend upon for survival.

2 · The struggle over the schools

*I*t's September 1971 and school is about to open. In Pontiac, Michigan, black children and their parents are excited and nervous. The Federal district court has ordered the city to bus 8,000 black children to all-white schools outside their neighborhoods to equalize educational opportunities.

A dynamite blast suddenly erupts at the Pontiac bus depot. Ten empty school busses are set afire and destroyed.

White racists have vowed that they will never allow black children to be bussed to all-white public schools, no matter what the Federal law says. On Labor Day, thousands of white parents and children stage a huge protest demonstration through downtown Pontiac, shouting menacing slogans.

Next day as school busses set out to pick up children in the ghetto areas, nine furious white mothers chain themselves to the gates of the bus yard, forming a human barrier to prevent the busses from leaving. Police move in, cut the chains and arrest the shouting women. The busses roll.

Picket lines of hostile white parents and children block school entrances as the busses arrive. They shriek insults and threats at the black children who are hurried through their lines by policemen. Inside the classrooms hardly a white student is to be seen. White parents have declared a boycott.

The boycott holds solid for two days. Then gradually students begin straggling back to classes. Prejudice loses out to parental

September 8, 1971. White school children demonstrate against bussing in Pontiac, Michigan.

(UNITED PRESS INTERNATIONAL)

fears that their children will fall behind in their studies. Soon attendance is almost back to normal.

Despite stormy resistance, Main Street, Pontiac, has lost its struggle with Washington over the right to run its local schools as it thinks best.

Although compulsory integration is now the law of the land, many parents, black as well as white, are opposed to it.

"I pay high taxes to support our local school," protested one white parent, "and I have a right to educate my children there. Why should I be forced to put them on a bus and send them to a dilapidated firetrap of a school miles away, in a dangerous neighborhood, while paying taxes for that neighborhood's children to be bussed to our own local school?"

"The whites don't want our children in their school, and we

don't want our children taught by white teachers," declared one black parent. "We want community control over our own schools. I want my children under a black school board, a black principal and black teachers. And I want the Government to give us adequate educational funds so that we can make our own schools the equal in every way of white schools."

Americans who favor integration feel that equal education will never be possible, however, until black and white students are scrambled together in the same schools, so that all benefit alike from good facilities and good teachers.

With the passage of the Fourteenth Amendment in 1868, many blacks felt that the equality of treatment under the law it promised to all citizens included the right of black children to attend white schools. But in 1896 the Supreme Court ruled that the Fourteenth Amendment "could not have been intended to abolish distinctions based upon color, or to enforce social, as distinguished from political, equality." All that any state had to do was to provide "separate but equal" facilities for blacks (*Plessy v. Ferguson*). The doctrine prevailed for fifty-eight years.

Texas was jolted when it established a small law school at Texas State University for blacks, in order to keep them out of the prestigious all-white University of Texas Law School. A black student sued, charging that the black law school was "separate and *un*equal." In 1950 the Supreme Court agreed that Texas had to provide him with the opportunity for a legal education equal to that of whites (*Sweatt v. Painter*).

On the same day the Court also decided that the University of Oklahoma could not compel a black graduate student to sit at a segregated desk in his classroom and library and eat at a special table in the university dining hall. Such restrictions, said the Court, crippled his "ability to study, to engage in discussions and exchange views with other students" (*McLaurin v. Oklahoma*).

The stage was now set for the most sweeping Supreme Court ruling of all governing education. By 1954 a new situation prevailed. As blacks flocked into the cities, whites had fled into the suburbs. City schools began to decay from lack of funds and an exodus of good teachers to the suburbs. Sociologists largely agreed that separate education could not possibly be equal, practically or psychologically.

"I went to one of those separate but equal schools down South," dryly observed civil rights leader Dick Gregory. "I don't know how old the textbooks were, but they sure kept me out of the Navy. If people wanted to sail off the edge of the earth—I sure wasn't gonna be one of them! . . . And those Southern history books! Do you realize I was twenty-two before I learned that Lincoln freed the slaves? I always figured Jefferson Davis had us out on probation!"

The case of *Brown v. Board of Education* came before the Supreme Court when a black minister named Brown in Topeka, Kansas, was refused permission to send his little daughter Linda to the all-white Sumner School instead of to the all-black Monroe School. The nine justices unanimously agreed to overturn the "separate but equal" concept which had been upheld ever since the Court ruling on *Plessy v. Ferguson* in 1896.

In his historic 1954 ruling, Chief Justice Earl Warren declared, "Today, education is perhaps the most important function of state and local governments. . . . It is doubtful that any child may reasonably be expected to succeed in life if he is denied the opportunity of an education . . . available to all on equal terms. . . . To separate them from others of similar age and qualifications solely because of their race generates a feeling of inferiority as to their status in the community that may affect their hearts and minds in a way unlikely ever to be undone. . . . Separate educational facilities are inherently unequal." The Court ordered Federal district courts to enforce public school integration in every state.

Many southern legislatures at once angrily claimed the right of "interposition"—the right to refuse compliance when Supreme Court decisions threatened a state's local institutions. "I've got as much right to interpret the Constitution," claimed Georgia's Governor Herman Talmadge, "as anyone in this country." Warren and his fellow justices were castigated as "a bunch of radical sociologists."

"I know that Southern people, by and large, will neither recognize, abide by nor comply with this decision," asserted Senator James Eastland of Mississippi. "We are expected to remain docile while the pure blood of the South is mongrelized by the barter of our heritage by Northern politicians in order to secure political favors from red mongrels in the slums of the East and Middle West."

Eastland encouraged the development of hundreds of White Citizens Councils in southern states to resist desegregation, telling them that the Supreme Court order was "part and parcel of the communist conspiracy to destroy our country."

Eventually these groups merged into the Citizens' Councils of America, dedicated to "the separation of the races in our schools and all institutions." Local branches were urged to intervene forcefully when necessary to block integration.

Governor James Coleman of Mississippi urged every southern legislature to keep passing new state laws requiring segregation and to keep fighting for them in the courts.

"Any legislature can pass an act faster than the Supreme Court can erase it," he explained.

When Clennon King, a black professor, applied for admission to the graduate school of the University of Mississippi, in 1958, he was whisked away from the registrar's office by state patrolmen, held secretly for two weeks, committed to an insane asylum for a month, then forced to leave the state. Governor Coleman boasted, "It shows that we know how to protect your [Mississippians'] rights in such a way that the Federal government could find no excuse for putting hands on the state of Mississippi."

To prod the reluctant southern states, in 1955 the Supreme Court issued a Desegregation Directive ordering all local authorities to make "a prompt and reasonable start" toward desegregating their schools "with all deliberate speed."

But almost 100 southern congressmen signed a manifesto vowing to use every legal means to overturn the *Brown* ruling. "We decry the Supreme Court's encroachments on rights reserved to the states and to the people," they declared. A 1956 resolution by the Georgia legislature held *Brown* null and void.

In Fort Worth, Texas, when three black children announced their intention to enter a white school in 1956, a mob of 400 men gathered to hang a black straw effigy, and offered knives to white children who promised to use them. The National Association for the Advancement of Colored People (NAACP) demanded protection for the black children from Governor Allan Shivers.

Instead he called out the Texas Rangers to protect the white people of the town, saying he would not "intimidate Texas citizens who are making orderly protest against a situation instigated and agitated by the NAACP." He added, "If this course is not satisfactory under the circumstances to the Federal government, I respectfully suggest further that the Supreme Court, which is responsible for the desegregation order, be given the task of enforcing it."

In 1957 President Eisenhower declared, "I can't imagine any set of circumstances that would ever induce me to send Federal troops . . . to enforce the orders of a Federal Court, because I believe that the common sense of America will never require it. . . . I would never believe that it would be a wise thing to do in this country."

But he was forced to call out Federal troops in Arkansas, Mississippi and Alabama to compel those states to allow black students to attend all-white schools. Before then, state requests for Federal troops had been made during fifteen domestic crises, and many had been denied. Most presidents believed that a local situation had to be extremely serious, with a breakdown of local law and order, before they felt justified in ordering Federal troops to intervene. It was ironic that Eisenhower, who deplored strong Federalism, felt compelled to do just that.

When nine black students sought to enter Central High School in Little Rock, Arkansas, in 1957, Governor Orval Faubus ordered the state National Guard to surround the school and keep them out, under the pretext of "preserving the peace." It was the first time since the Civil War that a governor had sought to challenge Federal law openly with the use of state troops. A mob was allowed to riot and threaten the black children, compelling their parents to take them home.

Shocked, Eisenhower warned Faubus, "In any area where the Federal government has assumed jurisdiction and this is upheld by the Supreme Court, there can only be one outcome: the state will lose. I don't want to see any governor humiliated."

Faubus at first agreed to permit peaceful integration, then changed his mind. Eisenhower angrily ordered Little Rock authorities to stop obstructing justice, and took the Arkansas National Guard out of Faubus' hands by putting it under Federal orders. Then he ordered regular Army troops into Little Rock to restore order and enforce integration. The black children returned to school behind Federal bayonets.

Georgia's Herman Talmadge, now a Senator, introduced a bill for a constitutional amendment to return control of the schools to local authority. "The people of Georgia will not comply with the decision of the Court," he warned. "It would take several divisions of troops down here to police every school building and then they wouldn't be able to enforce it."

In 1958 a conference of chief justices of state supreme courts voted 36 to 8 to censure the Warren Court for its vigorous exercise of Federal powers against the states. The Council of State Governments asked Congress to curb them.

With President John F. Kennedy in the White House, black applicant James Meredith won the right to enter the University of Mississippi. Governor Ross Barnett assured white Mississippians that he would "stand in the doorway" to prevent Meredith's admission. A mob of a thousand white men rioted violently when the applicant appeared, guarded by 200 Federal marshals.

Barnett secretly phoned Attorney General Robert Kennedy to ask him to order the marshals to draw their guns so that the Governor could show the mob he was backing down only under superior force. But only tear gas was used to break up the rioting in which two men were killed by mob gunfire, with many others wounded. Kennedy was forced to rush 16,000 Federal troops to restore order on the Oxford, Mississippi, campus.

The next southern governor to "stand in the doorway of the schoolhouse" was George Wallace who did so at the University of Alabama. This time there was no violence. By prearrangement, the temporarily federalized National Guard escorted black applicants to the university entrance. The general leading the troops then announced his "sad duty" to order Wallace to step aside, and the Governor did so with a great show of reluctance. It was a performance designed to arouse Alabaman fury against Washington.

Realizing that direct confrontation with the Federal government on the racial issue was a lost cause, many states hit upon a new technique for sabotaging integration. They passed laws establishing new qualifications for admission to public schools. Without mentioning race, the new state requirements managed to exclude almost all black students from white classrooms. In 1958 a Federal court upheld Alabama's right to do so "upon a basis of individual merit without regard to their race or color" (*Shuttlesworth v. Birmingham Board of Education*, 1958).

Many states abolished the free public school system and set up free private schools, using public funds. Other states slowed down integration by redistricting school zones to keep black children in ghetto schools. Still other states arranged for token integration, keeping the number of black children enrolled in any white school to a handful.

After ten years, and despite over 300 lawsuits since the historic *Brown* decision, only 6 per cent of the nation's 3,000,000 black students were attending integrated classes with whites; and the vast majority of these were outside the South.

Most segregation in the North was on the basis of *de facto* discrimination—not by law, that is, but by the practice of neighborhood schools, so that black children attended ghetto schools, while children in communities restricted to white housing went to all-white schools.

In 1963 a group of black Indiana parents sought to overturn the neighborhood school enrollment plan as discriminatory. The

In other cities blacks also protested, demanding a voice in school policy.
(ROGER MALLOCH, BLACK STAR)

Supreme Court ruled against them, holding that neighborhood schools had not been designed for the purpose of segregation, so that the real problem was one of restricted housing, not of restricted schools (*Bell v. School, City of Gary*).

One year later the Court struck down an attempt by the school board of Prince Edward County, Virginia, to abandon its public school system and make tuition grants to parents who sent their children to private white schools (*Griffin v. County School Board of Prince Edward County*).

By 1967 Federal circuit courts had ordered immediate integration at the kindergarten level of all schools in Alabama, Florida, Georgia, Louisiana, Mississippi and Texas. The U.S. Office of Education warned recalcitrant states that those which refused to obey the *Brown* law risked having their Federal aid-to-education grants cut off.

In February 1970 a dozen southern senators, led by John C. Stennis of Mississippi and Strom Thurmond of South Carolina, angrily demanded that the same Federal school desegregation guidelines be applied to northern as well as southern schools, including compulsory school bussing for integration.

Attempts by the Federal government to do this met with a storm of opposition in northern cities, from which many middle-class families had fled to the suburbs. The poorer whites left behind were furious at attempts to integrate their urban schools, fearing such integration as a first step in integrating the city's white neighborhoods.

The Canarsie section of New York, ninety-five per cent white, was thrown into a frenzy by a New York City Board of Education attempt to bus thirty-two black and Puerto Rican children from nearby non-white Brownsville into a Canarsie junior high school.

Thousands of white residents demonstrated angrily, demanding, "Preserve our community!" Boycotting six elementary and two junior high schools, they succeeded in closing them down and forcing the Board of Education to delay the bussing program. Black parents bitterly referred to Canarsie as "up South."

The Nixon administration sought reelection votes among the alienated white "silent majority" by opposing bussing for the sake of "racial balance" in the schools, on the theory that this was not required by the *Brown* ruling.

By 1973 the northern system of *de facto* segregation was still

consigning blacks and Puerto Ricans to overcrowded and dilapidated schools with poor teachers and poor facilities. New York
City had seventy-five elementary schools with more than ninety
per cent non-white enrollment. Indianapolis had thirty-eight such
schools. In Chicago, eighty-seven per cent of all students in the
city were black.

Disillusioned by the failures of northern integration, many
black parents demanded the right to control and upgrade ghetto
schools. They also protested the taxation system for public
schools that resulted in only $500 a year per pupil being spent on
ghetto schools, while suburban taxes provided up to $2,000 and
more per pupil for suburban schools. As long as the best schools
were not open to all on a fair basis, inequality of educational
opportunities would persist.

"The neighborhood school policy cannot be used as an
instrument to confine Negroes within an area artificially delineated," Supreme Court Justice Felix Frankfurter had warned in
1958, adding, "If it is so used, the Constitution has been violated
and the courts must intervene."

A different kind of Federal milestone in education had been
reached with the National Defense Education Act of 1958,
spurred by the appearance in the sky of the Russian satellite
Sputnik. Congress, shocked by this symbol of advanced Soviet
scientific technology, legislated a crash program of grants-in-aid
to high schools and universities to speed up science education
and research.

Opposing the Act in a 1960 election debate with John F.
Kennedy, Richard Nixon declared, "When the Federal Government gets the power to pay teachers, inevitably, in my opinion, it
will acquire the power to set standards and tell the teachers what
to teach. . . . Once you put the responsibility on the Federal
Government for paying a portion of teachers' salaries, your local
communities and your States are not going to meet the responsibility as much as they should."

Kennedy replied, "If the money will go to the States and the
States can then determine whether it shall go for school
construction or for teachers' salaries, in my opinion you protect
the local authority over the school board." His election led to
strong programs of Federal aid to education and even stronger
programs under his successor, Lyndon B. Johnson.

The Democrats viewed Federal aid as a means of equalizing educational advantages for children in low-income school districts where property taxes, the basis for support of the public schools, were too small for an adequate school budget.

By the time Richard Nixon came to office, education had been federalized to a vast extent, with public schools and universities looking to Washington for support and direction. Nixon reversed the trend by impounding Federal funds for education voted by Congress, leaving it up to school and college boards to seek their portions of general revenue-sharing funds given to the states. Financially crippled, many important educational programs were forced to shut down.

Washington and Main Street also dueled over the question of religious teachings and practices in public schools. In 1925 Thomas Scopes, a high school science teacher, was arrested for teaching evolution in defiance of a Tennessee state law that forbade it as creating "disrespect of the Holy Bible."

Scopes was defended by famous criminal lawyer Clarence Darrow, representing the American Civil Liberties Union (ACLU). The prosecutor was former Secretary of State William Jennings Bryan, who insisted that the Bible was the foundation of the American government. Any teaching of Darwinism contradicted the Bible, Bryan maintained, and destroyed the principles on which the nation was built. He upheld the right of the Tennessee legislature to pass an antievolution law for the benefit of Tennesseeans, regardless of what the rest of the country might think about Darwin's theory.

Darrow cited the First and Fourteenth Amendments to support Scopes's right to teach evolution, and quoted a worldwide galaxy of scholars and scientists who upheld Darwin. The local court found Scopes guilty and fined him $100, but on appeal, the Tennessee Supreme Court reversed the decision.

The right of local school boards to make provisions for student prayers has been fought repeatedly before the U.S. Supreme Court. In 1948 one parent challenged the right of an Illinois school board to release students from class to receive religious instruction on school property. Justice Frankfurter ruled, "The public school must keep scrupulously free from entanglement in the strife of sects. . . . In no activity of the State is it more vital to keep out divisive forces" (*Illinois ex rel. McCollum v. Board of Education*).

When the New York State Board of Regents developed a "nondenominational" prayer to be said each day in school, the Supreme Court ruled in 1962, "It is no part of the business of government to compose official prayers to be recited as a part of a religious program carried on by government" (*Engel v. Vitale*). Readings of the Lord's Prayer and the Bible were also prohibited in public schools.

Other bitter religious battles fought between Washington and Main Street have involved aid to parochial schools. Until the Nixon administration, the Federal government consistently maintained that public funds could be used only for public schools. Parents who sent their children to parochial schools charged that this was unfair, since if those schools closed, the public would have to pay increased taxes to open and operate new ones.

The Supreme Court has upheld a state law providing free textbooks for children in parochial schools (*Cochran v. Board of Education*, 1930); a state law providing transportation for parochial school students (*Everson v. Board of Education*, 1947); and a state law allowing release of students for religious teaching outside the school (*Zorach v. Clauson*, 1952). In the latter two cases, however, the Court emphasized that no tax could be levied to support any religious activities or institutions, nor could a state introduce any religious instruction or practices in a public school.

In 1972, when Pennsylvania and Rhode Island passed laws permitting the payment of salaries to lay teachers in parochial schools who taught nonreligious subjects, the Supreme Court outlawed these state laws as unconstitutional.

President Nixon, in an address to a national Catholic conference, promised that ways would be found to provide aid to parochial schools. New York and Pennsylvania passed laws awarding tax credits and repayment of tuition to parents of children attending private schools. But in July 1973 the Supreme Court branded these laws unconstitutional and forbade all public aid to the nation's 11,000 parochial schools.

Justice Lewis Powell cited First Amendment provisions

"which safeguard the separation of church from state and which have been regarded from the beginning as among the most cherished features of our Constitutional system."

Father Joseph P. Bynon, superintendent of Brooklyn's diocesan schools, called the ruling "a biased, twisted interpretation of the First Amendment."

Even with extensive Federal aid under Kennedy and Johnson, a soaring inflation made the cost of schools burdensome to most communities. A taxpayers' revolt developed among homeowners, who angrily voted down expanding school budgets. They demanded that other means of financing schools be found. The problem was aggravated by the forced closing of many parochial schools, dumping extra student loads on public schools.

Those who favored an even broader role for Washington in education argued that state and local governments were simply no longer able to finance education adequately. As for the alleged dangers of Federal control, thousands of school districts had been aided by Federal grants with no interference in matters of local policy, administration and personnel.

Federalists also pointed out that no one had ever questioned the freedom or integrity of such federally supported educational institutions as the Library of Congress, the U.S. Geological Survey, the National Observatory, the Smithsonian Institution, the National Archives and the National Gallery of Art. Denied Federal funds, none of these institutions would have come into existence to serve the public.

Those who wanted Main Street alone to assume full responsibility for our schools argued that it was fair to ask parents to pay for their own children's education, but not for the education of others. Insisting that a falling birth rate would create a surplus, not a shortage of classroom space, they also argued against increasing teachers' salaries, pointing out that teachers got a year's pay for nine months' work. And Senator Barry Goldwater warned that federalized education would "weaken the authority of the citizens and their communities."

But adequate state solutions to the problem seemed unlikely during the second Nixon administration, when Federal funds for schools were both slashed and tied up by the White House. In

August 1973 five states sued the Government, seeking a release of $20 million in Federal aid to education voted by Congress but withheld by the President. The courts found Nixon's impounding of the funds illegal and ordered them released to the states.

Earlier, the failure of state legislatures to replace the needed funds for education cut off by the White House had led to a day of national protest by the country's public libraries. They simultaneously dimmed their lights and sounded sirens to warn the American people that the lights of knowledge were in grave danger of being extinguished throughout the nation.

3 · *Who owes us a job or welfare check?*

*I*t's January 1971 and as a result of Government cutbacks on defense and space programs, more people are unemployed than at any time in the past ten years. Tens of thousands of professional men are on the street looking for any kind of job to meet piled-up family bills. Among them is William Scheirer, 33, of Washington, D.C., a professional economist who had been earning $18,000 a year with a research firm.

Preparing a résumé of his qualifications and experience, he mails out 531 job applications to firms throughout the country. He receives exactly one offer—and that for only a part-time job. With a wife and three children to provide for, he takes the only local job he can find.

William Scheirer, educated at Princeton, the London School of Economics and Massachusetts Institute of Technology, starts driving a cab.

A *Los Angeles Times* reporter asked one former aerospace executive, "What happens when your income drops from $327 a week to $65?" The reply: "We eat hamburgers and chili beans. My wife and I changed functions. She goes to work every day. I stay home and take care of the house and children."

Who owes you a living in a job you've been trained for? Is it the Federal government's responsibility to make jobs when the private sector fails to provide full employment?

Those who would have the Government step in as an employer

Aircraft employees listen as government cutbacks on defense and space programs are announced.

of last resort point out the need for low-cost housing, more clinics and hospitals, better county roads, new park systems, water purification plants and other important programs to improve the quality of life in America. Isn't it wiser and cheaper in the long run, they demand, to pay men for jobs in those fields than to keep them idle on welfare rolls?

Those who oppose having the Government guarantee jobs to everyone who wants to work argue that Washington is an inefficient, wasteful employer. Many of the jobs, they insist, would be useless "make-work," creating a huge Federal bureaucracy that would add to everyone's tax burden. They also argue that government-guaranteed employment would lead to socialism.

The Government as a source of jobs had political origins in the administration of Andrew Jackson ("To the victor belong the spoils"). Jackson, it is true, was not motivated by a desire to establish the Federal government as an employer of the needy, but only to build the strength of his Democratic party by rewarding faithful supporters, however illiterate and unqualified. From Jackson's time on, however, the Federal bureaucracy grew so rapidly that the government became an important source of employment, to the extent that public demand forced Washington to set up a civil service system to award such jobs on a merit basis fair to all. Today, fully 2,765,665 civilians work for the Federal government.

Like Jackson, Lincoln was also not backward in using his powers of patronage when he went to the White House in 1860. He appointed over a thousand of his supporters to Federal positions, and had to fend off thousands more disappointed job-seekers who vexed him with reproaches. After developing smallpox, Lincoln told his secretary, "Tell all the office seekers to come at once, for now I have something I can give to all."

Although jobs with the government were greatly sought after as prizes during most of the nineteenth century, few Americans thought of *demanding* such jobs as a right for the unemployed. The right to work was not considered a right in a period dominated by the spirit of "rugged individualism." A man was expected to find a job by his own determination, character, connections or union membership. The first important break in this tradition came in 1894, when a severe depression led Jacob Coxey to organize a national army of unemployed that marched on Washington to demand jobs.

Outraged by the invasion of "Coxey's Army," the House Committee on Labor refused to listen to Coxey's proposals. He and other marchers were arrested and given short prison sentences for "walking on the grass" and carrying banners. The first national movement to demand government jobs collapsed.

When World War I was followed by a depression, President Warren G. Harding rejected demands that the Federal government do something about providing jobs. "There has been vast unemployment before," he said, "and there will be again." Employment was a local responsibility, he insisted, and he called upon the mayors of America to assume it.

Following a stock market crash in 1929, which plunged the country into the worst depression in its history, the private operators of America's unplanned economy were unable to end the chaos. Between 1930 and 1932 over fifteen million people lost their jobs. Other millions received severe pay cuts. Most states had no unemployment compensation or public assistance programs, and there was no Social Security system.

Armies of men sold five-cent apples on street corners. In the coalfields of West Virginia, families evicted in midwinter shivered in tents. In Los Angeles people whose gas and electricity had been cut off were forced to cook over wood fires in back lots. A Philadelphia storekeeper who kept one family alive on credit told a reporter, "Eleven children in that house. They've got no shoes, no pants . . . no chairs. My God, you go in there, you cry, that's all."

In Chicago fifty men fought over a restaurant's back-door garbage. In Stockton, California, men scoured the city dump for half-rotted vegetables. In Salt Lake City hundreds of children were kept from school by the lack of clothing. In Harlan County, Kentucky, jobless miners and their families lived on wild greens, wild onions and other weeds. In Seattle jobless families without electricity spent every night in darkness or by candlelight. One New York City couple lived in a cave in Central Park for an entire year.

"Out of the ordeal of the Depression came damaging blows to the states," observed Governor Terry Sanford of North Carolina in 1960. "From the viewpoint of the efficacy of state government, the states lost their confidence, and the people their faith in the states."

In a helpless state of shock, the governors looked to Washing-

"Coxey's Army" on its way from Massillon, Ohio, to Washington.

(CULVER PICTURES, INC.)

New York City's unemployed built a village of shacks in Central Park.
(CULVER PICTURES, INC.)

ton to save their states. Yet in July 1932, when Congress passed the Wagner-Garner Act to let Federal employment agencies help states which had no such agencies, President Herbert Hoover vetoed it on grounds that it would interfere with the state control of employment.

As the Democratic candidate for President in 1932, Franklin D. Roosevelt insisted that only total Federal planning—a New Deal for "the forgotten man"—could provide jobs for everyone and get the country back on its feet.

Hoover denounced Roosevelt's promise to put ten million men to work as "a promise no government can fulfill." He labeled FDR's New Deal a "proposal of revolutionary changes which would undermine and destroy the fundamentals of the American system of government." If Roosevelt were elected, he warned, "the grass will grow in the streets of a hundred cities, a thousand towns. The weeds will overrun the . . . farms."

But desperate Americans no longer believed in the ability of businessmen and the states to look after their welfare. Elected by a landslide vote, Roosevelt set up a Public Works Administration (PWA) that spent over $3 billion on useful public works to "put the largest possible number of people to work."

The Civil Works Administration (CWA) built or improved half a million miles of roads, 40,000 new schools, over 3,500 playgrounds and 1,000 airports. Fifty thousand teachers were employed to keep rural schools open and teach adult classes.

Under the Federal Emergency Relief Administration (FERA), millions of people on welfare rolls were put to work erecting public buildings and bridges, clearing streams, dredging rivers, terracing land and running nursery schools for poor kids.

For the first time in American history, the Federal government also gave a vast subsidy to the cultural arts. Millions of Americans who had never seen a live play were able to see stunning productions put on at penny prices by the Federal Theater. Guidebooks on each of the states (still used today) were written by a Federal Writers' Project.

Young Americans who had despaired of a society where no one seemed to value or care about them were given their first jobs by a National Youth Administration. The NYA built TB clinics in Arizona, raised milking barns in Texas, landscaped parks in Michigan and renovated schoolhouses in North Dakota.

A Civilian Conservation Corps (CCC) gave jobs to over two million youths, aged eighteen to twenty-five, who worked in reforestation, road construction, prevention of soil erosion, national park and flood control projects. Youths who enrolled in the CCC lived in National Forest work camps and were paid $30 a month, part of which went to their parents back home.

The whole New Deal program was threatened in 1935 when a heavily conservative Supreme Court ruled in a key case that it was unconstitutional because it sought to exert Federal power over businesses that operated within state lines (*Schecter Poultry Corp. v. U.S.*). But with the aid of Congress, Roosevelt was able to reorganize New Deal agencies to make them legally invulnerable to Court nullification.

In 1941 he issued an executive order setting up the Fair Employment Practices Committee. The FEPC forbade all firms with government contracts to practice discrimination in hiring, guaranteeing blacks the same job opportunities as whites. Although the South strongly resisted the FEPC, within two years black employment had doubled in commercial and Navy ship-yards, while aircraft firms that had employed no blacks at all had been compelled to add a total of 5,000 on their payrolls.

The end of World War II revived fears of a postwar depression, so President Harry S. Truman won passage of the Full Employment Act of 1946. It affirmed Federal responsibility for providing "conditions under which there will be afforded useful employment opportunities . . . for those willing, able and seeking to work." A joint Federal-State Employment Service sought to locate jobs for the unemployed.

Although President Dwight D. Eisenhower opposed a strong role for Washington in providing jobs, under his administration millions of jobs were provided by an expanding military defense program sparked by the Cold War. Under the Kennedy adminis-tration, Secretary of Defense Robert S. McNamara sought to save a billion dollars a year by shutting down 862 unnecessary military bases. Many states protested vehemently.

Objecting to the closing of an armory at Springfield, Governor John Volpe of Massachusetts pointed out that it would add to the city's jobless poor while at the same time Washington was pouring out billions for an antipoverty program.

In 1964 President Lyndon B. Johnson persuaded Congress to set up an Office of Economic Opportunity (OEO) to provide Job Corps training programs for poor black and Puerto Rican youths. One year later he won passage of the Appalachian Regional Development Act, providing a joint Federal-state program of grants and aid to create jobs in the depressed Appalachian states.

In 1973 the Nixon administration shut off Federal funds for OEO, leaving it up to the states and cities to fund or drop OEO programs, as they wished, out of revenue-sharing funds. It was clear to most jobless Americans by this time that with Republi-cans in power, they would have to look to Main Street to provide jobs; and that with Democrats in power, they could expect Washington to try to put them on payrolls.

What about those for whom jobs cannot be found; those too ill or old to work; women without husbands who cannot work because they are forced to stay home and look after their children? Do they have a right to expect government support for themselves and their families? If so, who should be responsible for that support—Washington or Main Street?

Views on welfare divide the country. On one hand conservative taxpayers are indignant at abuses of the welfare system. Relief clients have been found secretly working and collecting fraudulent welfare claims. Some families on relief have managed to collect more money, and live better, than poor families with a working breadwinner. Some husbands have arranged to "desert" their wives, a fraudulent separation that allowed the wives to collect welfare funds in addition to getting money secretly from their husbands. Some able-bodied relief clients have refused work, preferring to live on relief out of laziness, dope addiction, etc. And some local welfare administrators themselves have been guilty of corrupt practices.

On the other hand liberal citizens tend to be indignant at hostile communities and states that keep poor families hungry and sick on stingy handouts, while spending lavishly on roads, sports stadiums and civic monuments. They also criticize a Federal military budget of over $80 billion for the Pentagon, while unfortunate men, women and children are compelled to live in grinding misery.

Ex-Senator Paul Douglas expressed concern over the values of Americans who grew furious at the news that a big-city family was cheating the Welfare Department out of $20 a week, while the same citizens shrugged at revelations that private companies were cheating the Government out of billions of dollars in overcharges—and for planes that could not fly.

In 1964 it was estimated that the number of individuals living on less than $3,000 a year—well below what the government itself had labeled "the poverty line"—accounted for up to thirty-five million Americans.

In early American times welfare was issued on a basis of pure charity. The poor, it was felt, were poor only because of a sinful flaw in their character. Their families bore responsibility for them; only if parents or children were unable to help were they entitled to relief. Then they had to take a pauper's oath, and their names were made public.

In the early nineteenth century the problem was negligible because jobs were plentiful in a rapidly expanding America. An

English immigrant to a village in western New York State wrote in 1828, "I have been poormaster of this town for many years, and I find it rare for a resident to become an annual town charge."

Expanding industrialization, a flood of immigration and the recurrence of depressions in the business cycle changed this picture. In 1847 the Irish potato famine brought such vast immigration to New York that almost a quarter of the city needed some form of public charity.

Congress passed a bill in 1854 to provide Federal public land for the use of states in caring for their impoverished insane. President Franklin Pierce vetoed the bill, insisting that Washington could not become "the great almoner of public charity throughout the United States."

In 1883 welfare worker Josephine Shaw Lowell branded relief evil because it allowed a man "to live in idleness and vice upon the proceeds of the labor of his industrious and virtuous fellow citizen." Even then the man without a job was viewed as a shiftless parasite; lack of jobs or frail health were not considered valid excuses.

Congress grew disturbed in 1889 by the unrestricted immigration flowing into New York City when "every charitable institution in the State of New York is now not only filled with occupants, but overflowing." Similar conditions prevailed in Pittsburgh, Boston and other cities. A committee appointed to study the problem discovered that many of the paupers in state institutions had also been paupers and convicts in Europe. Their passage had been paid by their own countries to transfer the cost of their upkeep to the United States. The committee called for Federal regulation of immigration which until then had been left up to each of the states.

"The regulation of immigration is a matter affecting the whole Union," said the committee, "and is pre-eminently a proper subject for Federal control." But because big business was booming and needed cheap labor, nothing was done. Even after two more depressions—in 1907 and 1914—the jobless kept arriving to swell the ranks of those willing to work for starvation wages. The luckless were forced to ask for charity.

When Congress finally passed an act establishing Federal regulation of immigration, Woodrow Wilson vetoed it in 1915 as a violation of American tradition. "The right of political asylum," said the President, "has brought to this country many a man of noble character and elevated purpose who was marked as an outlaw in his own less fortunate land, and who has yet become an ornament to our citizenship." Two years later, however, Congress succeeded in curbing immigration.

During the postwar depression of 1921 it was curtailed even more severely. President Warren Harding, urged to sponsor a Federal welfare program for the jobless, replied, "I would have little enthusiasm for any proposed relief which seeks either palliation or tonic from the public treasury." The conservative American Federation of Labor also opposed relief and even any form of Federal unemployment insurance.

The depression that followed the stock market crash of 1929 significantly changed American thinking when millions were forced, for the first time, to join breadlines in order to survive. Now it became clear that it was not the individual's fault that he had no job, nor the means to buy food, clothes and shelter for his family. It also became apparent that private charity could not possibly cope with an economic disaster of such magnitude.

States which tried to provide emergency funds found themselves rapidly going broke. *Today* magazine wired state governors to ask whether they were ready to have their states assume responsibility for relief. Only one of the thirty-seven who replied said that he was willing. Most governors made urgent appeals to the Federal government to come to their rescue.

Washington at first refused to heed. President Hoover simply appealed to industries to make more jobs available; and urged the rich to give bigger contributions to charity. He considered welfare payments destructive of initiative, and in any event the responsibility of local governments. But he finally agreed to Federal loans to the states for that purpose.

In the summer of 1931 Roosevelt, as governor of New York, called an emergency session of the legislature. "To these unfortunate [jobless] citizens aid must be extended by Government," he insisted, "not as a matter of charity, but as a matter of *social duty*." Winning a bill to set up a state relief program administered by local communities, he soon realized, however, that the problem far exceeded the resources of even a rich state like New York.

The demand for a Federal relief program was intensified by the Bonus March to Washington. Jobless veterans of the First World War insisted that they be kept afloat by payment of a long-promised war bonus. But the Bonus Army was driven out of Washington by Federal troops at Hoover's orders. Two veterans were killed; a baby died of tear gas; and the veterans' encampment was burned down. A shocked nation saw in such actions the same insensitivity to suffering that denied Federal relief to the poor.

Up to this point much welfare was being provided by big city political organizations. Precinct captains responded to the pleas of poor families by providing coal, warm clothing, baskets of groceries and talks to landlords to hold off on the rent. Grateful recipients of this largesse voted into office the choices of the ward politicians, who were repaid by opportunities to plunder city and state treasuries through graft. City bosses opposed Federal relief as diminishing their power, except insofar as they could be sure such welfare would be dispensed only through their hands and favor.

As president, in May 1933 Roosevelt pushed a bill through Congress authorizing a half billion dollars in relief, to be channeled by the Federal Emergency Relief Administration (FERA) through state and local agencies.

When one relief worker took a delivery of food, including pork, to destitute farm families in Michigan, he reported, "I had a hard time making some of 'em understand about the pork. Some thought I was trying to sell it to 'em, and when I said not, they wanted to know if it was really for them, and finally I sez it was a present from the Government. A lot of 'em—especially the old folks—broke down and cried. I guess all some of 'em has to eat is potatoes and beans and bread, and not any too much of that."

In 1935 FDR proposed a Social Security program designed to give Americans protection against unemployment, disability, widowhood, old age and special need.

"It would take all the romance out of life," protested New Jersey's Senator A. Harry Moore. "We might as well take a child from the nursery, give him a nurse, and protect him from every experience that life affords." Mississippi reaction was reflected in the Jackson *Daily News*: "The average Mississippian can't imagine himself chipping in to pay pensions for able-bodied

The Bonus Army arrived in Washington with high hopes . . .

but Federal troops and police broke up their encampment on President Hoover's orders.

A second generation of veterans—soldiers who fought in World War II—marched for jobs in 1946.

(WIDE WORLD PHOTOS)

Negroes to sit around in idleness on front galleries, supporting all their kinfolks on pensions, while cotton and corn crops are crying for workers."

Despite a conservative attack on the Social Security Act as a symbol of a "cradle-to-grave" welfare state, it was passed by a liberal Congress. The Act represented a giant step to aid the "one-third of a nation" which Roosevelt described as "ill-clothed, ill-housed and ill-fed."

As a concession to states' righters upset by the extent to which Americans were being taught to look to Washington for the solution of their problems, Congress in 1936 voted to transfer control of Federal relief programs to the states. Senator Harry S. Truman of Missouri declared, "I always acted on the theory that whatever could be adequately handled on the local, or state, levels should not be under the control of the Federal government, unless emergency conditions prevailed, as . . . during the early 1930s."

But in May 1938 FERA reported that black people in seventeen southern states were being kept on the edge of starvation by local welfare officials who expected families of six to live on $13 a week. Many black families began fleeing North to get on more generous relief rolls. Soon millions migrated.

Some thirty years later Mayor John Lindsay complained, "As the burden of welfare continues to grow northern cities like New York must scrimp on other absolutely crucial services. . . . New York City and New York State must bear the full financial burden of their Home Relief Program."

The New York State legislature imposed welfare limits that provided only sixty-six cents a day for feeding a child; under $100 a year for all a family's clothing and furniture; and nothing for a telephone or recreation of any kind. Replying to critics of welfare, Lindsay asked, "How many would regard that kind of sustenance as a prize to be wrested from the taxpayers?"

Some states sought to prevent an influx of poor blacks, Puerto Ricans and Mexicans from outside the state onto their relief rolls—which were only partially subsidized by Federal funds—by making a year's residence mandatory before anyone could apply for welfare. In the 1960's the Supreme Court invalidated such laws as restricting the right to move freely around the nation.

In 1964 President Johnson called for "unconditional war on poverty in America." But civil rights leader Bayard Rustin denounced his Great Society program as a mere "bag of tricks." And critics charged the Federal bureaucracy with bungling.

Charles Schultz, Budget Director under Johnson, admitted, "When it comes to aid to programs in education, pollution, manpower, poverty, health, and urban renewal, it is no longer possible to sit in Washington and operate them effectively."

President Nixon's program of New Federalism advocated decentralization and emphasis on states' rights, while proposing a substitute for welfare programs—the Guaranteed Annual Wage. Under this plan every family would be guaranteed a minimum income. Breadwinners would be forced to accept "suitable" jobs offered, and any families whose earnings fell below the minimum would be paid the difference by the U.S. Treasury.

"Let's quit subsidizing those who are able to work, can have jobs or could get them and refuse to take them," the President declared. But Congress argued over how large a minimum Guaranteed Annual Wage the country could afford to pay, and Nixon quickly let his proposal fade as election rhetoric.

"The average American is just like the child in the family," he told a *Washington Star* reporter. "If . . . you make him completely dependent and pamper him and cater to him too much, you are going to make him soft, spoiled and emotionally a very weak individual." This view underlined his slashing of Federal social programs, to compel citizens to look for solutions to their problems at a local level.

"Welfare and unemployment for Nixon are not so much social problems," observed M.I.T. historian Professor Bruce Mazlish, "as they are moral problems."

A runaway inflation in 1973 and 1974, added to unemployment due to the energy crisis, increased the distress of the nation's poor families, with the war on poverty still an unsolved problem to challenge the next generation of American leaders.

In 1968 the Reverend Ralph Abernathy led a Poor People's March on Washington to dramatize the plight of minority peoples.

(ROBERT HOUSTON, BLACK STAR)

4 · Who protects your civil liberties?

*I*t's 1940 and the patriotic spirit in America is running high because of the threat from the Rome-Berlin-Tokyo Axis. The Nazis have just invaded France. In a West Virginia community, patriots are outraged when the children of Jehovah's Witnesses refuse to salute the American flag, because their religion forbids them to recognize "any graven image."

Public indignation compels the children's expulsion. The Witnesses fight the case to the Supreme Court. Does a compulsory show of patriotism outweigh their freedom of conscience?

"If there is any fixed star in our constitutional constellation," rules Justice Robert H. Jackson for the majority, "it is that no official, high or petty, can prescribe what shall be orthodox in politics, nationalism, religion, or other matters of opinion, or force citizens to confess by word or act their faith therein. . . . We think the action of the local authorities in compelling the flag salute and pledge transcends constitutional limitations on their power and invades the sphere of intellect and spirit."

He adds pointedly, "The very purpose of the Bill of Rights was to withdraw certain subjects from the vicissitudes of political controversy, to place them beyond the reach of majorities and officials." Significantly, this bold decision is delivered in 1943, with the United States now at war (*West Virginia Board of Education v. Barnette*).

A cartoon of 1798 depicts a battle between Federalist Roger Griswold and Republican Matthew Lyon in the halls of Congress.

(THE BETTMANN ARCHIVE, INC.)

The first major assault on civil liberties in our history came not from a state but from the Federal government itself. In 1798 the Adams administration secured passage of the Alien and Sedition Acts, giving the President the right to jail and fine his critics for circulating "false, scandalous, and malicious" opinions about the government or its officers.

Outspoken anti-Federalists were dragged through the streets to court and jailed in Vermont, Pennsylvania, Virginia and Kentucky. The new laws were denounced by the Virginia and Kentucky Resolutions. Speaking for Virginia, Thomas Jefferson argued that since the Constitution gave the Federal government no powers of censorship, "all lawful powers respecting the same did of right remain, and were reserved to the States, or to the people." Speaking for Virginia, James Madison declared, "The liberty of conscience and of the press cannot be cancelled, abridged, restrained, or modified, by any authority of the United States."

The Federalists accused Jefferson and Madison of fostering

treason and government by newspaper. "Were it left to me to decide whether we should have a government without newspapers, or newspapers without a government," Jefferson replied, "I should not hesitate a moment to prefer the latter."

As soon as he was elected, he declared the Alien and Sedition Acts null and void. "I discharged every person under punishment or prosecution under the sedition law," he wrote in July 1804, "because I considered, and now consider, that law to be a nullity, as absolute and as palpable as if Congress had ordered us to fall down and worship a golden image."

The problem of civil liberties has often been a bone of contention between Washington and Main Street throughout our history as a nation. When Andrew Jackson came to the White House in 1829, he brought with him a frontier suspicion of unbridled Federal power. His views were reflected in an 1833 Supreme Court decision by Chief Justice Marshall holding that the Bill of Rights was binding only upon the Federal government, not upon any state government (*Barron v. Baltimore*).

Many northern states felt their sovereignty invaded by Washington through the Federal Fugitive Slave Act, which deprived them of the right to protect runaway slaves within their own borders. Abolitionist editor Sherman M. Booth, violating the law, was convicted by a Federal district court in Wisconsin. He appealed to the state Supreme Court and was freed, but the case went to the U.S. Supreme Court where his conviction was reaffirmed. The state was told it had no business interfering in a Federal case. An angry Wisconsin legislature passed a resolution defending state sovereignty against Federal intrusion.

Pennsylvania legislators banned the forcible seizure and removal of a fugitive slave. When a test case reached the Supreme Court in 1842, Justice Joseph Story's decision straddled the issue of Federal versus state power. He ruled, first, that the state law was unconstitutional. But he also ruled that since executing the Fugitive Slave Law was a Federal responsibility, no state had to take any part in enforcing it (*Prigg v. Pennsylvania*). Taking the hint, northern states quickly passed "personal liberty" laws forbidding any state officer to help capture or return a fugitive.

Although the North vigorously upheld the right of states to oppose slavery within their borders, despite Federal law, it was quick to deny states' rights when cited by the South to defend the right to secede from the Union. After the Civil War destroyed both the Confederacy and slavery, the defeated South bitterly resisted the reimposition of Federal power. Throughout the Reconstruction period, white southerners connived to regain control of their state legislatures. When they finally succeeded, they were swift to sabotage black rights.

They were helped by an 1873 Supreme Court decision in which Chief Justice Samuel Miller drew a fine distinction between the rights of blacks as American citizens and as citizens of a particular state. The Fifteenth Amendment, he ruled, did not prevent "the deprivation of their common rights by state legislation" (*Slaughterhouse Cases*). The civil rights of southern blacks were thereafter left to the questionable mercies of their state and local officials.

"Let there be White Leagues formed in every town, village and hamlet of the South," demanded an 1874 editorial in the *Atlanta News*. "We have submitted long enough to indignities, and it is time to meet brute-force with brute-force."

The Ku Klux Klan terrorized black voters and officeholders, while southern legislatures, courts, businessmen and police officials conspired to reduce them to second-class citizenship. In an effort to stop this sabotage of the Fourteenth Amendment, Congress passed the Civil Rights Act of 1875. But two years later Southern politicians struck a deal with President Rutherford B. Hayes that made all Federal laws protecting black Americans in the South dead letters.

Freedom of the press was the issue when public officials in Minnesota shut down a newspaper under a state law forbidding publication of "malicious, scandalous and defamatory" material. That the editor could prove his charges of official corruption was held immaterial. When the case went to the Supreme Court in 1931, Chief Justice Charles Evans Hughes declared the Minnesota law unconstitutional. The First Amendment guaranteeing a free press would be meaningless, he held, if any paper or magazine could be shut down for publishing stories a government deemed obnoxious (*Near v. Minnesota*).

Similarly, the Court struck down a subsequent attempt by Governor Huey Long of Louisiana to tax an opposition newspaper out of existence (*Grosjeans v. American Press Co.*).

Free speech was equally inviolate to Justice Hughes. In 1937 when a Communist named De Jonge called a public meeting to discuss a public issue, he was arrested and convicted in Oregon under a state criminal syndicalist law. Hughes overturned the conviction, declaring that public meetings to discuss needed social changes was what America was all about, no matter who called such meetings or what was advocated.

During the 1930s Jersey City Mayor Frank Hague, political boss of New Jersey, boasted, "*I am the law!*" He forbade meetings and speeches by anyone he deemed radical or undesirable. His police intimidated the owners of halls, set up road blocks, searched out-of-town cars and ran any "undesirables" out of town. Labor leaders were frequently beaten up, arrested and jailed for creating "riots and disturbances." Among those deported from Jersey City were Socialist leader Norman Thomas and ACLU counsel Arthur Garfield Hays.

In 1939 the Supreme Court made it firmly clear that the Constitution applied even to Jersey City, ruling that "the privilege of a citizen of the United States to use the streets and parks for communication of views on national questions may be regulated in the interest of all; it is not absolute . . . but it must not, in the guise of regulation, be abridged or denied" (*Hague v. C.I.O.*).

Norman Thomas under arrest in New Jersey.
(UNITED PRESS INTERNATIONAL)

The CIO and other organizations long banned by Hague then held an open-air meeting in the center of the city. Hague's goon squads were kept at bay by the same city police who had so often clubbed down such demonstrations. Norman Thomas was even escorted to the speaker's platform by Hague's Chief of Police, who now asked meekly, "Is everything all right, Mr. Thomas?"

Democracy had come to New Jersey.

After World War II, a Chicago court convicted one Father Terminiello of inciting to riot by making an inflammatory pro-Fascist speech. The Supreme Court overturned his conviction as Justice William O. Douglas explained, "A function of free speech under our system of government is to invite dispute. It may indeed best serve its high purpose when it induces a condition of unrest, creates dissatisfaction with conditions as they are, or even stirs people to anger."

Reversing a similar California conviction, Justice Louis Brandeis agreed with Douglas and added, "The remedy to be applied is more speech, not enforced silence."

During the Cold War, angry passions led many state legislatures to pass antisubversive laws. Pennsylvania tried and convicted Steve Nelson, an acknowledged Communist, under a state sedition law. When he appealed in 1956, the Supreme Court ordered him freed on grounds that sedition was a Federal, rather than state, matter for legislation and enforcement.

Chief Justice Earl Warren pointed out that total confusion, as well as double jeopardy, would result from the attempt of forty-three states with sedition laws to prosecute those also subject to Federal prosecution (*Pennsylvania v. Nelson*). Over thirty-five state attorneys general indignantly branded the Court's decision "dangerous to public safety."

In 1957 an applicant to the California bar refused to answer questions by state bar examiners about his past political affiliations. He was refused a license to practice because of doubts about his "moral character and loyalty." The Supreme Court compelled California to admit him to the bar, holding that his rejection had violated his Federal right to take the Fifth Amendment (*Konigsberg v. State Bar of California*).

Alabama and Washington collided head-on over the First Amendment in 1963. Three years earlier Dr. Martin Luther King's followers had placed an ad in *The New York Times* criticizing Alabama state and local officials. Montgomery Commissioner L.S. Sullivan had sued the *Times* for libel, winning a $500,000 judgment from the Alabama Supreme Court.

The U.S. Supreme Court reversed the judgment, holding that Sullivan had failed to prove deliberate malice and that freedom to comment on official conduct was in any event protected by the First Amendment. To reward such libel suits would result in "a pall of fear and timidity imposed upon those who would give voice to public criticism." The Court rejected "the Alabama concept of libel" as an "extraordinary restraint imposed on discussion of public issues."

During the antiwar, civil rights turmoil of the 1960s, many angry state legislatures sought to discourage dissent among teachers and other public employees by compelling them to take state loyalty oaths—a practice that had had a vogue since the outbreak of Cold War hysteria in the 1950s. In Washington state, faculty members of the state university refused, then fought their discharge up to the Supreme Court. They won on grounds that such oaths were "unconstitutionally vague" (*Bagget v. Bullitt*, 1964).

When a Quaker teacher challenged Arizona's loyalty oath requiring public employees to swear that they were not members of the Communist Party or any organization advocating violent overthrow of the Government, the Arizona Supreme Court ruled against her. But in 1966 the U.S. Supreme Court reversed that decision. Justice Douglas branded the oath law unconstitutional because it was based on the doctrine of "guilt by association" (*Elfbrandt v. Russell*).

The Court also struck down New York State's Feinberg Act, under which "subversive" teachers were subject to arbitrary firing (*Keyishian v. Board of Regents of the University of the State of New York*, 1967). This ruling was the final nail in the coffin of state loyalty oaths, which Justice Hugo Black called "the implacable foes of free thought."

But Main Street, upset by anti-Vietnam demonstrations and urban riots, put pressure on Washington for Federal "law and order" legislation. Senator Strom Thurmond of South Carolina proposed the Anti-Riot Act of 1968, making it a Federal crime to travel across state lines with the intent of inciting or organizing a riot. Attorney General Ramsey Clark objected in that riot control was a local problem and that Washington should not prosecute demonstrators but protect their First Amendment rights of free speech and assembly against arbitrary punishment as "rioters" by local officials.

"Let's forget the First Amendment!" snapped Louisiana congressman F. Edward Hébert. Congress passed the bill, which was used by the Nixon administration to prosecute the Chicago Seven, the Black Panthers and other dissenters—prosecutions that were usually overthrown by higher courts.

Washington and Main Street are frequently at odds over laws establishing standards of morality. In Alaska two Seward teachers were fired for "immorality" because they dared criticize the local school board and superintendent. Alaska's Supreme Court upheld the conviction, but in 1965 the U.S. Supreme Court ruled it a constitutional violation.

In the same year the High Court struck down a Connecticut antibirth-control law, and established a new constitutional "right of privacy" for doctors and patients.

New York and Maryland legislatures, offended by increasing sexual frankness in films, passed strict film censorship laws permitting the banning of controversial films where exhibitors could not prove they were moral. The Supreme Court struck down these state statutes on grounds that it was up to a prosecutor to prove that such films were "utterly without redeeming social value," rather than to assume them pornographic.

But a flood of hard-core pornography in films, books and magazines greatly upset Main Street, which demanded that local censorship be permitted. In June 1973 the Supreme Court, now more conservative with four Nixon appointees, bowed to Main Street by reversing its former position.

"People in different states vary in their tastes and attitudes," wrote Chief Justice Warren Burger in a new ruling, "and this diversity is not to be strangled by the absolutism of imposed uniformity." The whole issue of morality was turned back to state and local authorities, who were now given the power to decide their own community standards of obscenity.

The ruling created consternation among publishers and film producers. Each film, book and magazine could now be separately judged—and separately banned—by fifty different states and thousands of local communities. To increase the confusion, what could not be read or seen in one town was obtainable simply by traveling a few miles to where it was permitted.

In his dissenting opinion from the Court's ruling, Justice William O. Douglas saw it as a serious threat not only to freedom of expression and the right of Americans to see or read what they wished, but also to the very liberty of those whose ideas of morality offend local censors. "To send men to jail," he warned, "for violating standards they cannot understand, construe and apply is a monstrous thing to do."

Washington and Main Street have clashed over the exercise of local police power in ways that violated civil liberties. In 1929 the National Law Enforcement Commission appointed by President Hoover found that city police regularly used force and fear to coerce confessions, isolating and beating suspects until they confessed. In St. Louis suspects were "sent around the Horn"— held incommunicado and transferred every few days from one precinct to another for relentless grilling ("the third degree") to force a confession.

During the late 1930s Florida sheriffs rounded up forty black tenant farmers without a warrant, threw them in the county jail and kept them awake day and night for a week until they agreed to confess to a crime of murder. None was allowed to contact friends, families or counsel. Their conviction by Florida's courts was thrown out by the Supreme Court in 1940, on grounds that confessions elicited under such conditions violated the very essence of individual liberty.

"They who have suffered most from secret and dictatorial proceedings," ruled Justice Black, "have almost always been the poor, the ignorant, the numerically weak, the friendless, and the powerless. . . . Due process of law, preserved for all by our Constitution, commands that no such practice as that disclosed by this record shall send any accused to his death."

Minorities have often accused local police of disregarding constitutional rights in their zeal for prosecution. During World War II a Supreme Court decision affirmed the right of Jehovah's Witnesses to distribute antiwar leaflets. Later the same year the police of West Jefferson, Ohio, stopped them again when they tried. "We don't care for the Supreme Court," snapped one infuriated policeman, "and the Constitution don't apply here!"

In many states the poverty of defendants kept them from receiving the full justice of the law. An Illinois prisoner claiming errors at his trial was denied a transcript of the court proceedings because he could not afford to pay for it. The Supreme Court reversed his conviction on grounds that Illinois was wrong in refusing to furnish a copy of the transcript at public cost. "There can be no equal justice," the Court ruled, "where the kind of trial a man gets depends on the amount of money he has" (*Griffin v. Illinois*, 1956).

Until 1961 almost half of all state courts refused to outlaw illegally obtained evidence. Federal courts held such evidence inadmissible because it violated the Fourth Amendment regulating the right of search and seizure. Local police often searched suspects, their homes and personal effects at will, maltreating some in the process.

When this happened in an Ohio case, the Supreme Court finally ruled in 1961 that Federal standards for search and seizure also applied to the states. Otherwise, warned Justice Tom Clark, "the ignoble shortcut to conviction left open to the state tends to destroy the entire system of constitutional restraints on which the liberties of the people rest."

Washington and Main Street concepts of justice collided again in the case of a suspect kept in jail until he agreed to answer police questions. Subsequently convicted on a confession, he appealed to the Supreme Court, which freed him on grounds that no state had the right to ignore the Fifth Amendment's protection against self-incrimination. Justice William J. Brennan held that there could not be two standards of justice for Federal and state proceedings, because "the American system of criminal prosecution is accusatorial, not inquisitorial" (*Malloy v. Hogan*, 1964).

History was made by fifty-one-year-old Skid Row denizen Clarence Gideon, who had already served time for four felonies when he was arrested for burglarizing a poolroom in Panama City, Florida. Too broke to afford a lawyer, he requested that the court provide one. But Florida law required the court to do so only in cases of capital crime. So Gideon conducted his own defense, lost the case and was sentenced to five years in jail.

From behind bars he wrote a penciled note to the Supreme Court requesting a review of his conviction because Florida had denied him the absolute right of counsel given to all penniless defendants in Federal courts. In 1963 the Court set aside his conviction. "In our adversary system of criminal justice," ruled Justice Black, "any person hailed into court who is too poor to hire a lawyer cannot be assured a fair trial unless counsel is provided him. This seems to us to be an obvious truth" (*Gideon v. Wainwright*). In a new trial with a court-appointed attorney, Gideon was found innocent.

The Supreme Court's *Gideon* decision exploded like a bombshell throughout the country. Legislatures and courts in twenty-three states quickly expanded or improved their court systems to provide counsel for all poor defendants. Florida was compelled to release 1,300 prisoners who had been convicted without benefit of counsel, retrying only 300 whom it felt could be reconvicted.

Less than a year later the Supreme Court delivered another landmark civil liberties decision in the case of Danny Escobedo, 22, who was arrested by Chicago police for the murder of his brother-in-law. Before letting him consult a lawyer, the police interrogated him until late at night, without informing him of his Fifth Amendment right to remain silent. Confessing, he was convicted by an Illinois court, but then was set free after an appeal to the Supreme Court.

"We have learned," wrote Justice Arthur Goldberg, "that a system of criminal law enforcement which comes to depend on the 'confession' will, in the long run, be less reliable and more subject to abuses than a system which depends on extrinsic evidence independently secured by skillful investigation" (*Escobedo v. Illinois*, 1964). All state courts must now refuse to consider confessions obtained by police from an accused person when he is not represented by counsel.

Although the Fifth Amendment gives a defendant the right not to testify at his trial, six states permitted prosecutors to comment upon such a failure to take the stand, influencing a jury to consider it a silent admission of guilt. In one such case in California, the defendant was convicted of first-degree murder. But the Supreme Court overturned the verdict. Justice Douglas ruled that state prosecutors may not "solemnize the silence of the accused into evidence against him" (*Griffin v. California*, 1965).

Another important Fifth Amendment decision was rendered in the case of Ernesto A. Miranda, a twenty-three-year-old Mexican-American accused of raping an eighteen-year-old girl. After she picked him out of a police line-up as her assailant, Arizona police interrogated him without informing him of his rights to silence and a lawyer. At first denying the charge, Miranda finally wrote out and signed a confession.

Convicted and sentenced to up to thirty years in prison, he appealed on grounds that the police interrogation had violated his Fifth Amendment right to keep silent. In 1966 the Supreme Court agreed, even though no force or threat of force had been used to obtain the confession. A suspect subjected to "incommunicado interrogation in a police-dominated atmosphere" was, in effect, being "compelled to bear witness against himself." His conviction was overturned (*Miranda v. Arizona*).

The *Miranda* decision aroused a storm of protest from states' rights advocates, who accused the Supreme Court of tying the hands of local police in the face of a rising crime rate. "The Supreme Court has become obsessed with this overemphasis of individual rights," charged Senator Robert Byrd of West Virginia, "as against the rights of society."

The American Civil Liberties Union expressed an opposite concern because of the extension of Federal authority into local law enforcement. In 1972 Federal narcotics agents swooped down on a suspect, Dirk A. Dickenson, in an illegal helicopter raid on his cabin in Humboldt County, California. When they charged at him without identifying themselves, he fled in fright and was shot down in the back. In 1973 other narcotics agents in the Midwest twice burst into wrong homes without warrants, terrorized innocent victims, then withdrew after realizing their mistake. Local courts had no jurisdiction over Federal agents in pursuit of their duty, however mistakenly.

Law enforcement procedures are complex because often there is a thin dividing line between the authority of Federal and state or local agencies. The authority of the FBI is limited to about 600 statutes affecting Federal matters, so that most law enforcement is left to state and local governments. The question of who is responsible for protecting civil liberties is frequently confusing.

In 1973 local police stood by while Ted Patrick, a self-proclaimed specialist in restoring runaway young people to their homes, helped a young woman's parents abduct her from a Jesus cult, then held her in restraint while he "deprogrammed" (disillusioned) her about the cult. The ACLU demanded that the state's U.S. Attorney probe such kidnappings, but he insisted that they were family matters in which the FBI should not interfere. New York law enforcement authorities were finally compelled to arrest Patrick on charges of assault and unlawful imprisonment, but a jury acquitted him.

In March 1974 a jurisdictional dispute arose over prosecution of the chief Watergate defendants accused of obstruction of justice and a long series of civil liberties violations. If both California and the Department of Justice prosecuted the defendants on the same charges, they would be placed in double jeopardy. The State of California decided to yield prosecution of the case to the Federal prosecutor because of the national significance of Watergate.

The American political system operates something like the Army's chain of command. To demand your rights under the U.S. Constitution, it is first necessary to seek them at a lower level. If they are included in your state constitution, the interpretation and implementation of those rights is up to the state's courts first, subject to appeal to Federal courts.

But Washington reporter Stewart Alsop notes, "By using the Fourteenth Amendment boldly to extend the reach and power of the Bill of Rights, the Warren Court has deeply altered the whole delicate relationship between the federal government, the states, and the individual citizen."

The Bill of Rights protects every citizen from invasion—by Federal, state or local government—of the right to free thought, speech, press, religion, association and protest. At times threats to those rights have come from city administrations, county bosses and state legislatures; at other times from the Federal government itself, as in the Watergate revelations about the Nixon administration's secret plans to violate the rights of those on its "political enemies" list.

The Bill of Rights has never been a popular document with the majority of Americans on Main Street, precisely because the Founding Fathers intended it to protect the minority from the majority. George E. Reedy, President Johnson's press aide, once observed that if the American people ever called a constitutional convention, "it will probably be for the purpose of abolishing the Bill of Rights and restricting the authority of the judiciary."

"Historically," observes historian Henry Steele Commager, "federal centralization has not appeared to be the most notorious threat to the liberties of the citizen. . . . Attacks upon liberties guaranteed in bills of rights have come from states rather than from the nation."

It is the very nature of civil liberties that they are the rights of *all* Americans, protected in the last analysis by the Constitution. They cannot be limited or rescinded by any state, even if ninety-nine per cent of the people of that state are determined to deprive a minority of those rights.

5 · Who can take us to war?

Anger flares through the campus at Kent State University in Kent, Ohio, when President Nixon announces in May 1970 that he is widening the Vietnam War by sending troops into Cambodia. Students organize peaceful protest rallies that last until midnight, when town police seek to break them up. A few hotheaded radicals smash store windows, and the following evening firebomb an ROTC building on campus.

Prodded by indignant townspeople, Mayor Leroy Satrom asks Ohio Governor James Rhodes to call out the National Guard. Declaring martial law, the Governor accompanies an armored regiment and an infantry battalion into Kent. He brands the antiwar demonstrators "the worst type of people that we harbor in America," and pledges, "We are going to eradicate the problem. . . . It's over with in Ohio." Forbidding all campus assemblies—peaceful or otherwise—the Governor vows that the troops will remain on campus all year if necessary.

Indignant antiwar students gather for a noon rally as hundreds of others amble from classes to lunch. A campus police official demands that the demonstrators disperse. When they refuse, the Guard moves against them with fully loaded M-1 rifles at the ready. Tear-gas grenades are hurled into the demonstrators' ranks. Some students hurl objects back.

Without warning, Guardsmen open fire directly into the crowd of students. Shrieks and moans fill the air as four students fall

Kent State, May 5, 1970.   (UNITED PRESS INTERNATIONAL)

dead. Nine others are wounded. Not one has been closer than
seventy-five feet to the troops who later insist that they had felt
threatened. Tears of outrage stream down the cheeks of horrified
student witnesses. "Butchery!" cries twenty-nine-year-old graduate student William Fitzgerald.

A thousand members of the Kent State faculty meet and
resolve, "We hold the Guardsmen, acting under orders and under
severe psychological pressures, less responsible for the massacre
than are Governor Rhodes and Adjutant General Del Corso,
whose inflammatory statements produced these pressures."

Kent State president Robert I. White orders the university
closed for the rest of the semester and asks for a high-level
investigation. The Department of Justice conducts an inquiry
which finds the handling of the Guard largely to blame.

The father of Allison Krause, one of the slain students, asks
bitterly, "Have we come to such a state in this country that a

young girl has to be shot because she disagrees with the actions of her government?"

But Main Street, Ohio, supports the Vietnam War and is intolerant of dissent. A Portage County grand jury, instead of indicting any Guardsmen or state officials for the tragedy, indicts twenty-five members of Kent State's student body and faculty for the disturbances. The grand jury issues such a prejudiced report that a U.S. District Court judge, on appeal, is compelled to order it destroyed and stricken from the record. And the state is later forced to drop charges against twenty defendants.

Feeling that it is hopeless to expect justice in the matter from any Ohio state court, Allison Krause's father files a civil suit against the state in a Federal court for the wrongful death of his daughter. The court holds, however, that the Guardsmen responsible acted as agents of the state, and as such, are technically immune to suit in a Federal court.

Attorney General John Mitchell refuses to bring them before a Federal grand jury on charges of violating the dead and injured students' civil rights, claiming a lack of evidence. But after his resignation and the development of the Watergate scandal, a Department of Justice anxious to restore its credibility admits that such evidence *does* exist. In January 1974, almost four years after the Kent State killings, it is presented to a Federal grand jury in Cleveland, and a number of Guardsmen are indicted. In addition, the Supreme Court authorized the parents of the wounded and slain Kent State students to sue the Governor of Ohio and the National Guard for damages.

Main Street has not always been so vehemently supportive of Washington's wars. In fact, during the early stages of our history as a nation, Main Street more frequently challenged the Federal government's right to wage war and conscript troops for it.

Those states that had been only lukewarm about voting for the American Revolution balked constantly at providing troops and supplies for George Washington's army. He was disgusted by the quality of the state militia that did reach him, referring to them as "men just dragged from the tender Scenes of domestick life . . . ready to fly from their own shadows." He added caustically, "No reliance, except such as may arise from necessity, should ever be had in them again."

After the Revolution, Congress rejected Federalist demands for a standing army as an unnecessary tax burden and a threat to civil liberties. "Give [Secretary of War Henry] Knox his army," warned Pennsylvania Senator William Maclay in 1790, "and he will soon have a war on hand." Indian warfare compelled Congress to authorize a Federal force of 5,000 men two years later, but kept control of them in state hands.

George Washington authorized the use of the state militia to curb "combinations too powerful to be suppressed by the ordinary course of judicial proceedings." In plain language—to put down insurrection in any state. That challenge came in the summer of 1794 with the so-called Whisky Rebellion along the Pennsylvania western frontier. That state's farmers, who could not get their grain easily to market, depended upon distilling it into alcohol. Fiercely opposed to a Federal tax on whisky, they fought off Federal marshals collecting it.

Washington and Alexander Hamilton viewed this revolt as a challenge to the authority of the Federal government that had to be met lest it spread to other states. They asked Congress for authority to call out 15,000 state militia. Pennsylvania Governor Thomas Mifflin asked dubiously, "Will not resort to force inflame and cement the existing opposition?"

But the militia were raised in four states and led against the whisky farmers by Hamilton in uniform. He took 150 prisoners, marching them through Philadelphia at bayonet point. Only two were jailed, however, and Washington pardoned both.

The crushing of the Whisky Rebellion put all states on notice that no Federal decrees could be resisted. Jefferson's Democrat-Republicans were deeply resentful of this subordination of state authority. When Jefferson became president, he resolutely opposed raising a Federal army. Despite deteriorating relations with England and France, he declared, "I am for relying . . . on our militia solely, till actual invasion."

Ironically, the Federalists of New England viewed Jefferson's broad exercise of presidential powers as an even greater threat to states' rights—at least, to *their* states. They suspected his Louisiana Purchase as a plot to add states to the agrarian South, at the expense of the industrial North. Meeting secretly in 1804 with New York and New Jersey Federalists, the New Englanders argued for secession.

A Federal inspector is tarred and feathered by Pennsylvania farmers in the 1794 Whisky Rebellion.

When Jefferson sought to stop British and French attacks on American shipping by his Embargo Act, he enraged New Englanders once more. Their mercantile trade with the British badly crippled, they accused Jefferson of exceeding his constitutional powers. Massachusetts Governor Jonathan Trumbull called upon other New England governors "to interpose their protecting shield between the rights and liberties of the people and the assumed power of the general government." They refused to enforce the Embargo Act until a U.S. district court upheld the Federal government's right to proclaim it.

When President James Madison went to war with England in 1812, it was over the bitter opposition of the New England states. They refused to permit their militias to serve outside state territories. "If your sons must be torn from you by conscription," the Massachusetts legislature told citizens, ". . . let there be no volunteers except for defensive war."

The New England states also withheld their money from a war that destroyed their commerce while laying open their coastal towns to British naval attack. They were indignant when Secretary of War James Monroe asked Congress in 1814 to authorize a Federal draft of 80,000 state militia for two years.

In a resolution attacking the draft bill, the Connecticut legislature protested, "Our sons, brothers and friends are made liable to be delivered *against their will, and by force,* to the marshals and recruiting officers of the United States, to be employed, not for our own defence, but for the conquest of Canada."

The bill passed in the Senate, but Daniel Webster cried in the House, "Where is it written in the Constitution . . . that you may take children from their parents . . . and compel them to fight the battles of any war in which the folly or the wickedness of the government may engage it?" The bill failed.

At secret sessions of the Hartford Convention in 1815, the New England states once more deliberated over whether to secede from the Union if Washington did not pledge to respect states' rights to oppose such wars in the future. But this concept was dealt a blow in 1827 when the Supreme Court ruled that the President, acting under congressional authority, was the sole judge of the existence of emergencies under which the militia might be federalized for war use, and that his decision was binding on all state officials (*Martin v. Mott*).

When Andrew Jackson came to the White House in 1829, he attacked compulsory militia duty as undemocratic, since rich men could evade it by simply paying a fine. State musters ceased to be enforced, and the militia dwindled to small companies of volunteers who got together for social occasions.

In May 1846, when President James Polk decided to seize California and the New Mexico territory, he declared war on Mexico as a pretext. The New England states vehemently opposed "Mr. Polk's War" as a scheme for adding slave states to the Union. To reduce popular resistance, Polk did not call up any state militia, fighting the war instead with regular army volunteers.

The Massachusetts legislature resolved nevertheless that it was both a Christian and patriotic duty "for all good citizens to join in efforts to arrest this war." To set an example of civil disobedience, Henry Thoreau refused to pay his state poll tax and went to jail, rather than contribute a penny that might be used to support an unjust war.

When secession finally came, however, it was not New England but the southern states which seceded, believing that Lincoln's election in 1860 would doom the slavery on which their economy and society was based. Jefferson Davis, President of the Confederacy, declared that since the power of the Federal government stemmed only from a compact among the states, any state had the right to end that agreement and form a new compact.

In his first inaugural address, Lincoln sought to soothe the southern states by assuring them, "I have no purpose directly or indirectly to interfere with the institution of slavery in the States where it exists." And he acknowledged, "This country, with its institutions, belongs to the people who inhabit it. Whenever they shall grow weary of the existing Government, they can exercise their *constitutional* right of amending it or their *revolutionary* right to dismember or overthrow it."

Changing the Union was one thing; but destroying it completely was another: "Whence this magical omnipotence of 'State rights,' asserting a claim of power to lawfully destroy the Union itself? Physically speaking, we cannot separate. . . . A husband and wife may be divorced and go . . . beyond the reach of each other, but the different parts of our country cannot do this. They cannot but remain face to face, and intercourse either amicable or hostile, must continue between them."

When South Carolina's shore batteries opened fire on the Federal outpost of Fort Sumter, Lincoln called out the militia of all nonrebellious states to "suppress" the rebels. Volunteer state regiments were raised under the command of officers chosen by the governors. Responsibility for clothing, equipping and promoting troops was kept in state hands.

Treasury Secretary Salmon P. Chase, reflecting popular sentiment, refused to attempt to raise a purely national army to fight the Civil War. "I would rather have no regiments raised in Ohio," he declared, "than that they should not be known as Ohio regiments."

Southerners loyal to both state and nation found themselves faced with a painful choice. When the governor of Virginia asked Robert E. Lee to lead that state's troops in the Confederate Army, he wrote sadly to a friend, "With all my devotion to the Union . . . I have not been able to make up my mind to raise my hand against my relatives, my children, my home. I have therefore resigned my commission in the Army."

Northern and border states were not without suspicions of Lincoln's assumption of special wartime powers, especially when he suspended the right of habeas corpus, permitting the arrest and detention without warrant or hearing of civilians by military orders. In Unionist Maryland, secessionist John Merryman was arrested by the Army on charges of destroying railroad bridges. When Chief Justice Robert B. Taney issued a writ of habeas corpus requiring Merryman to be brought to court to determine the justice of his detention, the Army refused.

Charging that Lincoln's suspension of habeas corpus was unconstitutional, Taney indignantly accused him of substituting military for civilian government (*Ex parte Merryman*, 1861). The Maryland legislature protested to the governor on account of his failure to protect the state's citizens against Federal oppression. Lincoln simply ignored the *Merryman* opinion.

Claiming inherent "war powers," he federalized the state militias as ninety-day volunteers, and increased the regular Army and Navy by 23,000 and 18,000 men respectively.

"In the interval between April 12 and July 4, 1861," noted historian William Dunning, "a new principle thus appeared in the constitutional system of the United States, namely, that of a temporary dictatorship. All the powers of government were virtually concentrated in a single department, and that the department whose energies were directed by the will of a single man." In June 1861 the editors of thirteen New York City newspapers passed a resolution denouncing the militaristic policies of the Federal government.

When Lincoln found it necessary to draft conscripts in March 1863, angry New York mobs tore through the streets sacking and burning Federal draft offices and arsenals, killing firemen and

Draft rioters plundered houses and stores in New York City in 1863.
(THE BETTMANN ARCHIVE, INC.)

policemen, looting stores, lynching blacks, attacking abolitionists and raiding pro-Union newspaper offices.

Newly elected Democratic governors Horace Seymour in New York and Joel Parker in New Jersey bitterly denounced the draft, and the use of martial law and arbitrary arrests, as violating America's traditional freedoms. Nothing in American history had prepared the citizenry to accept so extensive an imposition of militarism. A total of 13,000 civilians were held as political prisoners during the Civil War, most without trial or after only cursory military hearings.

In 1864 a notorious Copperhead (Southern sympathizer), Clement L. Vallandigham, was arrested in Ohio by General Ambrose Burnside, under Lincoln's Executive Order permitting the court-martial of all civilians accused of "disloyal practises." Governor Seymour angrily charged, "The arrest will not only *lead* to military despotism, it *establishes* military despotism!" Vallandigham's petition for a writ of habeas corpus was denied. On appeal, the Supreme Court now cautiously refused to review the case on grounds that its authority did not extend to the consideration of military proceedings.

Aware that he was on shaky legal ground, however, Lincoln freed Vallandigham from military prison, ordered him exiled to the South and warned Burnside against "unnecessary arrests and military trials." But the issue came to a head later that year in Indiana, where Lamdin P. Milligan was arrested by the Army on charges of conspiracy, and sentenced to hang by a military commission. This time the Supreme Court faced the issue squarely, holding that suspension of habeas corpus was unconstitutional, since the Indiana civil courts had been open and operative.

"The Constitution of the United States is a law for rulers and people, equally in war and in peace," ruled the Court, "and covers with the shield of its protection all classes of men, at all times and under all circumstances" (*Ex parte Milligan*, 1864).

In the Reconstruction period following the Civil War, an argument raged over whether the Southern states needed to be "re-admitted" to the Union, or whether they had never really been out of it since their secession had been unlawful.

In 1869 the Supreme Court was called upon to rule on the legality of actions taken by the Confederate state of Texas during

Children of men imprisoned for resisting World War I demonstrate for amnesty.

the Civil War. "The Constitution . . . looks to an indestructible Union, composed of indestructible states," said Chief Justice Salmon Chase. Since secession had been illegal, Confederate state authorities had never legally existed, and therefore their acts had been null and void (*Texas v. White*).

When Woodrow Wilson took the country into World War I, a Selective Service Act federalized National Guard units and authorized the drafting of a million men. Antidraft riots broke out in Montana, Michigan and Oklahoma. Challenged in the Supreme Court, conscription was upheld on grounds that the Federal government had the right to demand military service from its citizens as part of its sovereignty (*Arver v. U.S.*).

Skillfully orchestrated propaganda brought Main Street into line with Washington's war effort. When Congress passed Espionage and Sedition Acts to crack down on antiwar radicals, state legislatures competed by passing their own even more punitive versions. Both Federal and state agents raided Socialist, pacifist and labor groups, sweeping thousands off to jail in a wholesale disregard of constitutional rights, not only during but after the war.

The 1920s brought disillusionment with the war, however, and a demand by the states that Federal military power be cut back to prewar size. When the Navy Department sought to arouse popular fervor with a celebration of National Navy Day, half the nation's governors refused to sponsor it.

During the Second World War, the state of Texas balked at gas rationing by Washington. Why should Texans submit to this inconvenience, demanded Governor Coke Stevenson, when they had plenty of gas in their own back yard? He refused to set up rationing machinery until Federal OPA Administrator Leon Henderson flew to Texas to persuade him to enforce the law.

On a note of wry humor, Texans also ignored a wartime wood conservation directive reducing coffin lengths by three inches. They insisted that they were taller than most Americans and needed the full six feet six inches.

Later when Texas and Washington tangled over the rights to tidelands oil, Governor Price Daniels mobilized Texan owners of 286,000 pleasure boats to be "ready for emergency service at any time." He told the press he had "reactivated the Texas Navy as a patriotic organization to preserve the rights and boundaries of this state." Observed the *Dallas News*, "Daniels was quite serious about the whole thing."

Although the Constitution gives the power to declare war only to Congress, the United States emerged from World War II with presidential powers so greatly expanded that it was the White House, in one fashion or another, which began ordering American military forces into battle overseas.

President Truman committed American troops to fight in Korea in July 1950, when Russian-supported North Koreans invaded American-supported South Korea. Truman steamrollered a resolution through the United Nations calling for a "police action" to stop the aggression. The major U.N. forces sent to Korea under General Douglas MacArthur's leadership were American troops. No declaration of war by Congress was sought.

Subsequently President Eisenhower intervened with American troops in Lebanon in 1958 to fight off an alleged attack by Egyptian forces that proved a false alarm. President John F.

Kennedy mounted the Bay of Pigs attack against Castro's Cuba in 1961 and a year later sent a naval force to challenge Soviet ships bringing ballistic missiles to Cuba. Congress authorized neither of these warlike moves.

Then President Lyndon B. Johnson took the United States into a full-scale war in Vietnam by the ruse of a "Tonkin Gulf Resolution" he won from Congress after an alleged (and later disproved) attack upon a U.S. destroyer in the Gulf of Tonkin by three North Vietnamese torpedo boats. Johnson used the Resolution—"to take all necessary measures . . . to prevent further aggression"—as his authority to fight an undeclared war in Southeast Asia and to begin bombing North Vietnam in February 1965.

Rising disorders at home over the Vietnam War and the civil rights struggle led Johnson to order the use of Federal troops against civilian populations in Detroit, Baltimore, Washington and Chicago. The inability of local police to maintain law and order in these and other cities seriously weakened the arguments of those who insisted upon the supremacy of local power.

This became especially apparent in Chicago at the stormy Democratic National Convention of 1968, when Mayor Richard Daley's police indulged in what Johnson's own Presidential Commission later described as a "police riot" against antiwar demonstrators outside the convention hall.

Although the Vietnam War was widely unpopular, the states rigidly enforced draft laws and manifested hostility toward all antiwar protests as unpatriotic.

When high school students in Ohio wore black mourning bands to class to signify sorrow over the war, three who refused to remove them were suspended. In February 1969 the Supreme Court ruled that students were entitled to freedom of expression of antiwar views during school hours. Justice Abe Fortas added, "Students in school as well as out are persons under our Constitution. They are possessed of fundamental rights which the state must respect" (*Tinker v. School District*).

A Boston draft board refused to grant Harvard graduate John Heffron Sisson exemption as a conscientious objector because he opposed the war only on moral, not religious, grounds. Refusing induction in 1968, he was convicted of violating the draft law. His conviction was overturned in a U.S. district court, when

The Washington Coliseum was converted into a dormitory for some of the more than 13,000 demonstrators arrested in the antiwar protest of 1971.

Judge Charles E. Wyzanski held that it violated the First Amendment banning any law respecting an establishment of religion. State draft boards were compelled to grant a seventy-three per cent increase in C.O. classifications.

A Minneapolis draft board classified David Earl Gutnecht 1A for throwing his draft card at the feet of a Federal marshal at an antiwar rally. Labeled "delinquent" and drafted for it, he refused induction and was sentenced to four years in prison. But in January 1970 the Supreme Court reversed the decision, holding it unconstitutional for a draft board to use military service as a punishment for antiwar protest.

The one state which did oppose the Vietnam War was Massachusetts, where the legislature passed a bill in 1970 providing that the state's servicemen need not participate in a war that Congress had not declared. The Supreme Court ruled the Massachusetts law unconstitutional, but carefully avoided ruling on the legality of the Vietnam War.

In April 1971 it seemed as though Main Street itself—or at least its people—had come to Washington when antiwar leaders mounted a massive demonstration of 200,000 persons to protest

President Nixon's prolongation of the war. The administration quickly disrupted it by illegal arrests. In a single day 7,200 Americans were herded off into open-air, wire-fenced stockades, and in four days the total rose to 13,400—the largest mass arrest in the nation's history.

"Short of killing people," one administration official confided to *Newsweek*, "Nixon had given [Attorney General John] Mitchell a blank check." Hundreds of citizens caught in the mass arrests were innocent bystanders. The President called the roundup "a fine job." Almost all those arrested had to be released afterwards because of improper arrest procedures.

Loss of congressional support for Nixon's conduct of the war was a reflection of Main Street's disillusionment with all the promises of "light at the end of the tunnel" it had heard so often from the White House. "There is no question that the gradual shift of Vietnam sentiment from hawk to dove, first in the Senate and then more grudgingly in the House, was heavily influenced by constituent mail," observed *New York Times* Washington correspondent Warren Weaver, Jr.

This disillusionment was deepened by revelations in 1973 that the Nixon administration had secretly bombed Cambodia and Laos for three years, while the Pentagon falsified military reports and the President assured the American people that he was observing strict neutrality toward those nations.

The frequent readiness of the White House to take the country to war and to impose military laws upon the people has made Main Street increasingly wary of Federal power. The abuses of the presidency, revealed in the 1973 Watergate hearings, emphasized the importance of strengthening the traditional Constitutional system of checks and balances. In that year Congress stripped the President of the power to order American military forces into action outside the United States for longer than sixty days without the consent of Congress.

It seems unlikely that the Executive branch of government will be allowed again, for the foreseeable future at least, to wield unbridled power to the extent that it can operate as a virtual military dictatorship.

6 · Your voting power

The police of Greenwood, Mississippi, regard Douglas MacArthur Cotton as a serious threat to the security of their state. He and eight other black members of the Student Nonviolent Coordinating Committee are arrested, given a five-minute trial without permission to obtain an attorney, and convicted of "disturbing the peace." They are sentenced to $200 fines and four months at hard labor at the Leflore County Farm. Mistreated by guards, Cotton and the others go on a work and hunger strike in protest.

They are punished by transfer to Parchman State Penitentiary, where they are put in the "hot box"—a windowless, lightless closet—and kept there for two scorching days and nights. Several collapse. Later, Cotton is hung by his hands from the cell bars for three hours. He and the others are finally bailed out of Parchman after fifty-five days. A police sergeant warns Cotton that if he ever returns, he will be shot. Subsequently he is trailed wherever he goes by police who photograph and take the names of anyone he speaks to.

The frightful crime of which Douglas MacArthur Cotton had been guilty in June 1963, a crime against the state of Mississippi, had been leading 200 black citizens to the courthouse of Greenwood in an unsuccessful attempt to register to vote.

Most rules and regulations qualifying a person's right to vote are formulated by the states, and hardly any two states agree on requirements. You can be denied the right to vote in some public elections in California for fighting a duel; in Florida for betting; in Vermont for disorderly behavior; in South Carolina for being a pauper; in Idaho for not owning property; in Connecticut for not possessing a "good character"; and in Alabama for being illiterate. Until fairly recently nine states would not let you vote unless you could afford to pay poll taxes, including all accumulated taxes owed.

All kinds of bureaucratic rules have kept "undesirables" from voting. In Jackson Parish, Louisiana, for example, one black veteran was not allowed to register because he underlined instead of circling the designation "Mr." on a form.

Early in the Republic's history each of the states imposed severe restrictions upon suffrage, in order to keep power in the hands of an aristocracy of education, position and wealth. Citizens without property could not vote.

Acting through state legislatures, the elite carved up election districts with irregular boundaries drawn to magnify the voting power of small conservative districts, and shrink the voting power of large liberal regions. One rural district with only 400 residents, for example, would have the same representation in the state legislature, and in Congress, as a city district with 400,000. Election districts were also reshaped to combine special voting groups in such a way as to assure victory to the party doing the redistricting.

The practice was perfected under Massachusetts Governor Elbridge Gerry in 1812, when the state legislature divided Essex County into special voting districts. The boundaries of one had so curious a shape that a legislator suggested it resembled a salamander. Replied one wit dryly, "No, a Gerrymander." The name stuck to the political trick.

Property qualifications kept seventy-six per cent of New York State adult males from voting for their governor and senators. The state's election laws were democratized in 1821 at a Constitutional Convention, over the bitter protest of State Chancellor James Kent. "I wish to preserve our senate," he declared, "as the representative of the landed interest. . . . The tendency of universal suffrage is to jeopardize the rights of property and the principles of liberty. . . . There is a constant tendency in the poor to covet and to share the plunder of the rich."

But the forces of democracy were too strong. States in which the legislatures chose presidential electors began changing to the system of popular elections. Feeling their privileges threatened, the mercantile, landholding and banking classes sought to control elections by buying votes and voting dead men. During the 1837 elections, New York bankers spent $60,000 to buy the votes of ignorant immigrants. In 1848 convicts were brought from prisons to serve as repeat voters.

Although the Fifteenth Amendment in 1870 specifically guaranteed the vote to black citizens, southern states passed all kinds of laws to disenfranchise them on one pretext or another. They were aided by Supreme Court decisions which cancelled the Enforcement Act of 1870 by ruling that neither the Fourteenth nor Fifteenth Amendments was intended to destroy state control of elections. State officials were forbidden to bar blacks from approaching the polling place, but private individuals who did so were not covered by the ruling (*United States v. Reese*, 1876; *United States v. Harris*, 1883).

Withdrawal of Federal election officials from the South gave southern states a free hand in disenfranchising blacks. The chief devices they used were the literacy test, by which local officials in their discretion could ask difficult questions of "undesirable" voters; the poll tax, disqualifying most poor blacks; the "grandfather clause," which required a voter to have had an ancestor with the right to vote before 1866; and the white Democratic primary, which excluded blacks and guaranteed the election of white Democratic nominees in the one-party South.

The Supreme Court upheld literacy tests and poll taxes in 1898 (*Williams v. Mississippi*), but struck down the grandfather clause in 1915 (*Guinn v. United States*). White primary laws were allowed to stand until 1927, and even then the South continued to use modifications of them for still another fifteen years. The net result was that despite physical liberation from slavery, American blacks continued to be politically powerless for almost a century.

After the Supreme Court ruling that the Fourteenth and Fifteenth Amendments did not prevent private individuals from intimidating blacks from voting, the Ku Klux Klan needed no

Plan of the Contemplated Murder of John Campbell.

An 1871 drawing depicts the Ku Klux Klan preparing to lynch a supporter of black suffrage.

further encouragement. They initiated campaigns of mob terror, including burning crosses and lynching, to frighten blacks away from the polls. Congress then passed a law making it a crime for any individual to interfere with voting in Federal elections.

The Klan challenged the law as infringing on state control of elections. In 1884 the Supreme Court held that the right to vote stemmed from the Constitution and Federal laws, not exclusively from state laws (*Ex parte Yarbrough*).

But it was not until sixty years later that the Court firmly struck down the white primary law of the South, declaring that blacks could not be denied the right to vote in primaries (*Smith v.*

Allwright, 1944). This ruling ended the fiction that the Democratic primary was a private club's social function, rather than an indispensable part of the machinery by which state and Federal officials are elected.

Blacks were not the only minorities affected by *Smith v. Allwright.* Voters of Mexican extraction, too, had been denied a vote in the Democratic primaries. As a result of elections in which Mexican-American interests were never represented, no person of Mexican descent in Texas had ever sat on a grand jury, a trial jury or the bench. "I have been a newspaper man in Texas for 25 years," said Hart Stilwell of the *Texas Spectator* in 1946, "and . . . if an Anglo-American has served one day in the penitentiary for the killing of a Latin-American during that period of time, I have not heard of it."

Prevented from excluding minorities from primary elections, the Alabama legislature voted an amendment to the state constitution to give local officials unlimited discretion in deciding who was literate enough to vote. But in 1949 the Supreme Court ruled that the act was clearly designed to put the authority of the state behind the administration of unfair literacy tests, and so was unconstitutional (*Schnell v. Davis*).

Even more discriminated against at the polls of America, for almost a century and a half, was another minority—women. Not until suffrage rights had been won by large, formerly disenfranchised sections of the male population, was the question of women's suffrage even considered. In a male chauvinist society, it was taken for granted that only men were qualified to participate in "serious" matters like politics.

This discrimination against women cut across all lines—Federal, state and local. Prominent women like Lucretia Mott and Elizabeth Cady Stanton began the women's suffrage movement in 1848 by organizing the first Women's Rights Convention at Seneca Falls, New York. Out of this grew the National Woman Suffrage Association in 1869, with Mrs. Stanton as President and Susan B. Anthony as chairman of its executive committee.

But it was not until 1917 that the suffragettes, by persistent, militant campaigning, won their first important victory—an amendment to the New York State constitution giving women the vote. Two years later they compelled Congress to pass the Nineteenth Amendment to the Federal Constitution; it was

In 1913 suffragettes paraded in New York City, asserting that woman's cause was linked with man's.

ratified by three-fourths of state legislatures by August 1920, completing women's victorious struggle for enfranchisement.

During the New Deal era city voters grew increasingly disgruntled over the practice of state legislatures denying them proportional representation. Gerrymandering increased the power of rural areas unfairly. Chicago voters unsuccessfully sought to compel the Illinois legislature to divide the election districts according to population. The Supreme Court refused to intervene. "Courts ought not to enter this political thicket," said Justice Felix Frankfurter in 1946.

Some white citizens of Plaquemines Parish, Louisiana, were refused voter registration in 1953 by parish boss Leander Perez.

Their complaint to the Justice Department was rejected on grounds that it was a matter for the Louisiana Attorney General. But he in turn called it a local, not state, problem. Persistent complaints by black voters finally led the U.S. Senate Judiciary Committee to hold hearings on a bill to safeguard voting rights. Testifying, Perez angrily shouted that protecting black voters was both "un-American" and "communistic." Senator Everett Dirksen snapped, "That is as stupid a statement as has ever been uttered in this hearing!"

When civil rights workers planned to move into Plaquemines Parish to aid voter registration, Perez threatened to jail them all in a 200-year-old fort. Senator Russell Long complained, "People are getting tired of being called a communist just because they don't agree with you. . . . It's getting so it will be respectable to be called a communist!"

In 1957 Congress finally passed the Civil Rights Act enforcing the Fifteenth Amendment. The Federal government was given authority to go to court against any state, district, county, city, parish, township, school district or municipality which discriminated against any qualified voter and to institute contempt proceedings if court orders were ignored. A Federal Civil Rights Commission was established, empowered to investigate complaints and report to the President and Congress.

One group of blacks charged Alabama with gerrymandering the election district of Tuskegee from a square city boundary "into a strangely irregular 28-sided figure" which had the effect of "fencing Negro citizens out of Tuskegee." The redistricting excluded 396 out of 400 black voters, but not one white voter, keeping the city under total white control.

Lower courts upheld the right of Alabama to gerrymander Tuskegee. But in 1960 the Supreme Court rejected the state's claim of an unrestricted right to organize its own political subdivisions as the legislature saw fit. No state legislature, said Justice Frankfurter, could isolate "a racial minority for special discriminatory treatment" (*Gomillion v. Lightfoot*).

In 1962 the Supreme Court finally decided to intervene in state legislative reapportionment. Justice William J. Brennan ruled that under the Fourteenth Amendment, Federal courts had the power and duty to rule on the fairness of how state legislative districts were apportioned (*Baker v. Carr*).

The political implications of *Baker v. Carr* were enormous, affecting the whole question of how representative democracy should work. It laid the groundwork for another important Supreme Court decision when Georgia claimed that its county unit system of voting was no more unrepresentative than the election of the President by the Electoral College.

"The conception of political equality . . . can mean only one thing—one person, one vote," disagreed Justice Douglas in 1963. Otherwise, he pointed out, a resident of Georgia's smallest county would have ninety-nine times the political power and influence of a citizen of Atlanta (*Gray v. Sanders*).

Another Georgia case came before the Court in 1964 when the state legislature fought a challenge to its gerrymandering of congressional districts. Ruling that the Constitution required "equal representation for equal numbers," Justice Black ordered the challenged districts redrawn on a one-man, one-vote principle (*Wesberry v. Sanders*).

The *Gray* and *Wesberry* decisions promised to change the political character of both Congress and state houses across the nation. A dozen governors sought to stop Federal enforcement of democracy within their state boundaries.

"They do not want to see state governments invigorated, carrying through broad legislative programs," observed historian Henry Steele Commager, "they want to see the national government frustrated. . . . The ambition which animates them is not to strengthen the states, but to paralyze the nation."

In Birmingham, Governor George Wallace raised the cry, "Stand up for Alabama!" He called for unrelenting struggle against "the social engineers in Washington." A General Assembly of the Council of State Governments tried to establish a new "Court of the Union," composed of state justices, to function as a tribunal superior to the U.S. Supreme Court in all controversies involving Federal and state power.

But for all the uproar, the dike had broken irreparably, and democratic tides began pouring through. All over the country voters began challenging unfair districting systems used by state political machines.

In June 1964 the Supreme Court handed down a decision upholding all their challenges.

"Legislators represent people," declared Chief Justice Earl

Warren, "not trees or acres. Legislators are elected by voters, not farms or cities or economic interests. The resulting discrimination against those living in disfavored areas is easily demonstrable mathematically. Two, five or ten of them must vote before the effect of their voting is equivalent to that of their more favored neighbor. . . . Full and effective participation by all citizens requires . . . that each citizen has an equally effective voice in the election of members of his state legislature. . . . The fact that an individual lives here or there is not a legitimate reason for overweighting or diluting the efficacy of his vote" (*Reynolds v. Sims*).

All state legislatures were finally forced to begin reapportionment on a one-man, one-vote basis. District boundaries were redrawn to equalize the number of people in each election district, regardless of geographical size. When Louisiana sought to sabotage the new requirements by a statute requiring that the race of each candidate be designated on the ballot, the Supreme Court struck it down as obviously discriminatory and illegal (*Anderson v. Martin*, 1964).

But the Deep South continued to struggle against black suffrage. Civil rights workers from the South, joined by sympathizers from the North in voter registration campaigns, were often terrorized, beaten and sometimes murdered. "We're not going to tolerate any group from the outside of Mississippi or from the inside of Mississippi to take the law into their own hands," grimly warned Governor Paul B. Johnson.

Fannie Lou Hamer, a black militant, reported in 1964, "I tried to register in 1962. I was fired the same day, after working on the plantation for eighteen years. My husband worked there thirty years. When my employer found out I'd been down to the courthouse, she said I'd have to withdraw or be fired. 'We are not ready for this in Mississippi,' she said. 'Well, I wasn't registering for you,' I told her. 'I was trying to register for myself.' "

A voter registration drive was mounted in Lowndes County, Alabama, in the spring of 1965, because out of an eighty per cent black population of 15,000, not a single black had been registered to vote by March 1st.

During a civil rights protest march in Selma, the Rev. James Reeb, a thirty-eight-year-old white Boston minister, was beaten to death by a furious white mob. President Johnson appealed to

Civil rights marchers in Selma cross the Alabama River as state troopers stand guard.

Congress in a nationally televised address for a new civil rights bill guaranteeing black suffrage in the South.

"No law that we now have on the books . . . can insure the right to vote when local officials are determined to deny it," he pointed out. "In such a case our duty must be clear to all of us. . . . There is no issue of States rights or National rights. There is only the struggle for human rights."

The Voting Rights Act of 1965 suspended for five years literacy tests and other pretexts used to keep blacks out of the polls. Federal voting examiners were appointed for all voting districts where less than fifty per cent of the population was registered to vote. The U.S. Attorney General was ordered to test the constitutionality of all poll taxes in voting districts where they were apparently being used to disenfranchise blacks. Anyone who sought to intimidate a citizen from registering or voting was made subject to arrest on criminal charges.

For the first time Federal legislation really shook the South. Four states—Alabama, Mississippi, Texas and Virginia—sought to retain the poll tax. When the Attorney General brought suit in Virginia, the Supreme Court struck down the tax as violating the equal protection clause of the Fourteenth Amendment (*Harper v. Virginia Board of Elections*). South Carolina attempted to challenge the Voting Rights Act of 1965 as an infringement of states' rights. But the Supreme Court upheld its constitutionality in *South Carolina v. Katzenbach* (1966).

The effect of the Voting Rights Act in Mississippi was impressive. Before its passage there had only been 35,000 registered blacks in the whole state; after passage the number jumped to 200,000. By November 1967 they were strong enough to elect twenty-two blacks to public offices in the state, and throughout the South a total of 200 blacks took office.

The Supreme Court cracked down three times on the state of Florida for failing to submit an acceptable reapportionment law. The third time it criticized the "failure of the State to present . . . acceptable reasons" why some election districts had over fifteen per cent more voters than others.

"For decades the national Congress blinded itself to the gerrymandering activities of state legislatures," observed *The Nation* in April 1973. "For decades the Southern states supplied inferior schools for black children, and Northern states barred blacks from white neighborhoods. For decades police departments resorted to the third degree [against black suspects]."

Now, said *The Nation*, the Supreme Court's "vigorous reading of judicial obligations to enforce the equal protection clause of the Fourteenth Amendment" would give blacks at least a fighting chance to challenge such injustices at the polls.

It is understandable that minorities in the United States should have come to look upon Main Street as the enemy in their demand for a fair voice in local and national affairs. But they also felt betrayed by Washington when the Nixon administration, in deference to its southern supporters, showed a reluctance to enforce with any vigor the voting rights legislation they had struggled for and won during the sixties.

Despite this handicap, in 1973 such major cities as Los Angeles, Detroit and Atlanta elected black mayors for the first time in American history.

7 · *Tangling over taxes*

*F*or Demetrio Rodriguez, a twenty-eight-year-old Mexican-American laborer in San Antonio, Texas, the way in which local school taxes are used is of desperate importance. He has three sons for whom he has high ambitions. But he knows that the only way they will be able to climb out of the *barrio* is through an excellent education. And that's just what they can't get in the impoverished Edgewood School District where he lives.

In 1968 his district can raise only $37 per pupil from annual property taxes. In sharp contrast, across town the rich Alamo Heights School District is able to raise $412 per pupil—over eleven times as much. The situation is not unique to San Antonio. In New York for every $1 spent on pupils in the poorest public schools, $84 is spent on pupils in the best. In Kansas the contrast is a shocking $1 to $128.

Mr. Rodriguez believes that his children have the same right to attend the best public schools as children from rich homes and goes to court to fight for it. The San Antonio Independent School District insists that his children must attend their neighborhood school. At issue is the question of whether the prosperous communities of America, whose property taxes pay for the richest public schools, can reserve their use for their own children exclusively.

Sitting on the Supreme Court in April 1973 are four conserva-

tive new justices appointed by President Nixon. Joined by Justice
Potter Stewart, they rule that education is not one of the rights
specifically guaranteed by the Constitution. While admitting that
the Texas tax system is "concededly imperfect," they decline to
interfere with the use of local property taxes. The Court, Justice
Lewis F. Powell insists, should not rewrite state and local laws on
its own.

In an angry dissent, Justice Thurgood Marshall calls the
decision "a retreat from our historic commitment to equality of
educational opportunity." But it is understandably popular
among parents in well-to-do districts, who feel that if they are
willing and able to pay high property taxes for excellent public
schools, they should have the right to have their own children
benefit, rather than have those schools "invaded" by children
from poorer homes and neighborhoods.

Demetrio Rodriguez, hopes for his children's future crushed by
the Supreme Court's adverse decision, shakes his head and
observes sadly, "The poor people have lost again."

Because of President Nixon's cutbacks on Federal grants for
education, and because of an inflationary spiral that sent school
budgets soaring, a taxpayers' revolt developed in many school
districts. In Dayton, Ohio, ten school districts shut down their
schools in 1971 for lack of funds, after voters persistently rejected
school budgets. People complained that property taxes were
already so high that many were being forced to sell their homes.
Between 1962 and 1972 the nation's property taxes more than
doubled.

"The absurd overreliance on the local property tax," according
to R. L. Johns, director of the National Educational Finance
Project, is the cause of the problem. The President's Commission
on School Finance, pointing out that the quality of a child's
education depends largely on where he lives, advised that
property taxes should be replaced in part by statewide sales or
income taxes. Revenues should be divided equally among all
school districts, with the Federal government assuming a far
greater proportion of educational costs.

President Nixon did not agree with his Commission.

The Federal government relies heavily for its revenues on

income, corporation and excise taxes such as those on gasoline, liquor and telephone service. States derive sixty per cent of their revenue from sales taxes. Local governments collect eighty-seven per cent of their revenues from property taxes. Some cities also levy payroll and sales taxes.

All of these tax systems have inequities and loopholes.

Many Texas oilmen became millionaires because a twenty-seven and a half per cent "depletion allowance" (since reduced) allowed them to exempt that much of their income from Federal taxation. Some businessmen who earn over a million dollars a year have been able to pay nothing at all in taxes because of tax loopholes exploited by their accountants. In early 1974 Americans were shocked to learn that President Nixon had used these loopholes to avoid paying large taxes on his $200,000 salary and real estate profits. Yet an unmarried worker earning $125 a week has had to pay $13 of it to Washington, to say nothing of state income taxes and local property taxes.

Of all government taxes collected, Washington gets sixty-eight per cent, with state and local governments competing for the rest. Each level of government is immune to taxation by another level. Washington may not tax any bonds issued by states, counties, cities or school districts, or the interest paid to purchasers. In turn, no state may tax any Federal lands or operations which are within its borders.

Having become a nation because of bitter resentment against England for "taxation without representation," Americans have remained suspicious of the tax powers of the Federal government. When war with France threatened in 1799, Alexander Hamilton sought to raise new revenue through a direct Federal property tax. Tax collectors who went into Pennsylvania Dutch regions were forced to duck hot water poured on them from upper farmhouse windows by farmers' wives.

After marshals arrested some of the farmers, seven hundred Pennsylvanians led by former Continental Army officer John Fries forced their release. The marshals were driven off accompanied by cries of, *"Dämm de President, dämm de Congress!"*

In a show of Federal force, President John Adams sent a cavalry and artillery force of 2,000 militia from New Jersey. Fries was taken, tried for treason and sentenced to hang. Over

Hamilton's angry opposition, however, Adams pardoned him, an act that split the Federalists and let Jefferson win the White House.

At first Jefferson acted on the principle of taxing the people as little as possible. Centralized government, he believed, led to despotism. During his second term, however, he imposed taxes to finance internal improvements that states could not afford to fund themselves and that the nation's infant industries needed to expand and develop their markets.

In 1816 the state of Maryland decided to use its taxation powers to put a Federal project out of business. The project was the second United States Bank, bitterly opposed by state banks as a money monopoly. James McCulloch, secretary of the Baltimore branch, was ordered to pay Maryland a $15,000 tax and refused. In an 1819 Supreme Court decision, Chief Justice John Marshall upheld the Federal government's right to establish a National Bank as part of its "implied powers."

"If the states may tax one instrument, employed by the government in the execution of its powers," he declared, "they may tax . . . the mail . . . the mint . . . patent-rights . . . judicial process . . . which would defeat all the ends of government. This was not intended by the American people. They did not design to make their government dependent on the states."

Marshall added that no state had the right to tax the U.S. Bank because "the power to tax involves the power to destroy." The heart of the matter, he insisted, was "a question of supremacy," and no state could raise itself above the supreme law of the land (*McCulloch v. Maryland*).

Many states denounced the decision indignantly. But *McCulloch* remained a milestone ruling with implications far beyond the immediate tax question. By refusing to confine the Federal government to its powers as specified in the Constitution, Marshall made it possible for future Presidents to cope with new problems unforeseen by the Founding Fathers.

The high protective tariff, originally passed by Congress to protect budding home industries from overseas competition, became a source of conflict between Washington and Main Street when such protection was no longer necessary. Agricultural states of the South and West charged that it forced them to pay high prices for the manufactured goods of the North, while Northerners enjoyed the low prices of farm products.

When Congress ignored these complaints and passed another high protective tariff in 1828, enraged southerners labeled it the "Tariff of Abominations." John C. Calhoun, Vice President under Andrew Jackson, protested that it made southerners "serfs of the system." He supported South Carolina's threat to nullify the tariff and to secede from the Union if this right were denied her.

At a Jefferson Day dinner, President Jackson proposed a toast. Facing Calhoun, he declared firmly, "Our Union—it *must* be preserved!" Calhoun calmly countered with another toast: "The Union—*next* to our liberty, most dear!"

The South Carolina legislature resolved, "We will not submit to the application of force, on the part of the Federal Government to reduce this State to obedience. . . . We will consider the passage, by Congress, of any act . . . to coerce the State, shut up her ports, destroy or harass her commerce, to enforce the acts hereby declared to be null and void . . . as inconsistent with the longer continuance of South Carolina in the Union; and that the people of this State will thenceforth . . . organize a separate Government."

Jackson replied, "If South Carolina considers the revenue laws unconstitutional and has a right to prevent their execution in the port of Charleston, there would be a clear constitutional objection of their collection in every other port; and no revenue could be collected anywhere. . . . To say that any State may at pleasure secede from the Union is to say that the United States are not a nation. . . . Disunion by armed force is *treason*. Are you really ready to incur its guilt?"

South Carolinians answered that they owed their first allegiance not to Washington but to their state. They defied the President to show where the Constitution authorized him "to interfere whenever he may think fit, in the affairs of the respective states . . . with the sanction of force." Each state had "the right, whenever it may deem such a course necessary for the preservation of its liberties or vital interests, to secede peaceably from the Union."

The President angrily sent a warship and seven revenue cutters to Charleston harbor. He even wanted to go to South Carolina himself as head of a posse to arrest the nullification leaders and deliver them for trial. Governor Robert Y. Hayne defiantly issued a call for 10,000 South Carolinians to repel the Federal invaders. Congress passed the Force Act of 1833, empowering the Chief Executive to use force as necessary to execute Federal statutes within any state resisting them.

Conciliators rushed to defuse the explosive situation. With the worried assistance of Calhoun, Henry Clay worked out a compromise tariff that lowered the rates and eliminated some inequities. Meanwhile, South Carolinians found no other southern state willing to follow their lead. Given a face-saving excuse to avoid the dangerous confrontation of Federal versus state power, they accepted the compromise tariff.

The issues of nullification and the right to secede from the Union were far from settled, however. Postponed for a generation, they then provoked a far greater conflict.

In 1863 Congress was forced to set up a new Federal banking system to finance the Civil War. To hold down the supply of paper money and prevent inflation, a ten per cent tax was levied on state-chartered bank notes, while the Government paid its bills to soldiers, suppliers and the states with Federal greenbacks. The state banks, angry at having their paper money taxed out of existence, appealed to the Supreme Court.

In 1869 Chief Justice Salmon P. Chase upheld the Federal tax as a legitimate exercise of Congress's taxing power, and of its authority to provide for a sound national currency (*Veazie Bank v. Fenno*).

The growth of banking and industrial monopolies late in the nineteenth century led to the founding of great personal fortunes. Widespread resentment of the "Robber Barons," fanned by the Populist movement, compelled Congress to levy a two per cent Federal tax on all incomes over $4,000. Joseph H. Choate, lawyer for the Farmers' Loan and Trust Company, denounced the tax as part of a "Communist march."

In 1895 a Supreme Court sympathetic to big business ruled that since taxes on income from personal property were direct taxes, they were unconstitutional. So, too, were Federal taxes on income derived from state, county or municipal bonds. The Founding Fathers, said Chief Justice C. J. Fuller, expected the Federal government to meet its expenses primarily from indirect taxes such as sales, import and excise taxes, except in crises (*Pollock v. Farmers' Loan and Trust Company*). The ruling prevented any further attempt to collect Federal income taxes from the wealthy until the Sixteenth Amendment was passed in 1913 under Wilson.

Big business also managed to avoid most state and local taxes. "It is a notorious fact," declared the New York State Comptroller in 1900, "that hundreds of manufacturing companies, whose plants are located in this State, whose business is chiefly transacted here, and which for all practical purposes are New York enterprises, escape all indirect taxation in this State, and much local taxation, by being incorporated in other States." Yet New York was required to furnish them with the services of its firemen, police and other public facilities.

When New York's Governor Franklin D. Roosevelt campaigned for the presidency in 1932, he promised to cut both Federal taxes and expenditures to the bone. "We must eliminate unnecessary functions of Government," he declared, "functions, in fact, that are not definitely essential to the continuance of Government. . . . Let us remember well that out of every tax dollar in the average State in this Nation, forty cents enter the treasury in Washington, D.C." But almost as soon as he was elected, he embarked on the greatest Federal spending program the nation had ever seen up to that time, in order to provide welfare, jobs and economic recovery.

Roosevelt's magnification of Washington's role in large Federal spending remained in effect during the subsequent Democratic administrations of Truman, Kennedy and Johnson, with a hiatus during the Eisenhower years. In 1968 President Nixon sought to swing the pendulum back the other way, reducing Federal taxes, spending and financial control while returning a share of tax revenues and control over them to the states, along with responsibility for solving their own problems.

Calling his program the "New Federalism," he described it as a "new American Revolution" . . . a method of "returning power to the people." The President's plan for "revenue-sharing" was at first welcomed by many mayors and governors as providing them with the direct funds they desperately needed to solve multiplying municipal and state funds. But many soon complained that these funds were far less than the Federal programs they replaced which were cut from the budget.

When Congress realized this, it began voting special bills for Federal appropriations in education, health and welfare. President Nixon promptly impounded the funds Congress had authorized him to spend, declaring that to release them would be inflationary. Congressman Silvio O. Conte of Massachusetts introduced a bill to force him to spend the funds.

Conservative-Republican Senator James L. Buckley of New York told the author, "The President has challenged the Congress to face the issue of its frequently irresponsible budgetary decisions. . . . The cuts will be painful to some groups directly involved . . . [but] we will be more effectively coming to grips with the problems resulting from years of centralizing authority in Washington." Federal courts did not uphold the President's right to impound funds voted by Congress, however, and orders were issued commanding him to begin releasing them.

The majority of Americans on Main Street undoubtedly prefer local control and expenditure of tax funds. Minorities in most communities, however, usually find that Washington is more sympathetic to their needs—at least during Democratic administrations. Only when states and local communities fall upon hard times and are unable to cope piecemeal with grave financial problems does a general cry arise for the Federal government to step in with national financial solutions.

8 · Who looks after the minorities?

The nation is electrified in 1973 when 200 Indians suddenly seize the dusty prairie hamlet of Wounded Knee, South Dakota, where in 1890 U.S. cavalry troops massacred some 300 men, women and children of the Sioux tribe. The invaders belong to the American Indian Movement (AIM), determined to remind white America not only of that crime, and of 371 Indian treaties broken by Washington, but also of the Government's present-day mistreatment of tribes on the reservation.

The Oglala Sioux are bitter at the control of tribal council meetings by the Bureau of Indian Affairs (BIA) and charge the BIA with supporting corrupt tribal chiefs who give ninety-nine-year leases on valuable Indian lands to white entrepreneurs. AIM blames Washington for the fact that less than twenty per cent of the Oglala Sioux finish high school and less than half have jobs. Although the Federal government appropriates an average of $8,000 for every Oglala family, only $1,900 ever reaches each family. AIM claims misuse of tribal funds.

"There is no tribal self-government for Oglalas," charges the Indian newspaper *Wassaja*. "There is government by dictatorship." Hence AIM's seizure of Wounded Knee, declaring it an independent Oglala Sioux nation at war with 300 FBI agents and Federal marshals representing Washington. The Government blockades all roads leading into town and seeks to starve out the besiegers, rather than risk the embarrassment of organizing a second Massacre of Wounded Knee.

"The Government has two choices," declares AIM leader Russell Means, a young Oglala Sioux born on the reservation. "Either they attack and wipe us out like they did in 1890, or they negotiate our reasonable demands." He and other young braves vow their readiness to die for their cause.

Exchanges of gunfire kill two Indians and wound one FBI man seriously. Intermediaries promise a Presidential Commission hearing of all Indian complaints in Washington, if the besiegers give up their arms. After holding Wounded Knee for over two months, Means and the other Indians finally agree. They are arrested and indicted for violating the Riot Act.

In January 1974 the Department of Justice brings them to trial, hoping to keep all mention of Indian grievances out of the proceedings. But AIM has hired William Kunstler, who defended the Chicago Seven, as counsel, and Kunstler is determined to read into the record all the treaties with the Indians that the Federal government has broken. Meanwhile, Washington has

Indian militants escort a government agent from a meeting with the leaders of the Wounded Knee garrison, March 19, 1973.
(UNITED PRESS INTERNATIONAL)

broken another promise—to set up a Presidential Commission to hear all Indian complaints.

Nothing has changed for the Indians.

"Violence may be the only alternative to the Indians' problem," observes Sakokwanonkwas, a leader of the Mohawk Nation. ". . . . No leader of an Indian nation advocates violence, but one has to protect his people and his land and his children."

Indians also have long memories about injustices suffered at the hands of states. In 1828, for example, when Georgia settlers discovered gold on Cherokee lands, the state legislature obligingly nullified a Federal treaty and made the lands available to white settlers. The Cherokee Nation appealed to the Supreme Court. Chief Justice Marshall upheld Georgia on grounds that the Cherokee Nation could not be considered a separate foreign state (*Cherokee Nation v. Georgia,* 1831).

Alabama and Mississippi were not slow in following suit to seize the lands of the Choctaw and Chickasaw.

On the other hand, when a Georgia law sought to establish the state as the supreme authority in Cherokee territory, Marshall struck it down as usurping the powers of the Federal government (*Worcester v. Georgia*). Georgia's angry legislature defied the ruling, supported by President Andrew Jackson, who snapped, "John Marshall has made his decision. Now let him enforce it!"

In 1835 when 14,000 Cherokees refused to surrender their lands in Georgia and emigrate west to a new Federal reservation, the President sent General Winfield Scott and 7,000 troops to drive them there along the "Trail of Tears"—a harsh route marked by the graves of 4,000 who died on the way.

"There is a strong and growing feeling in this country," said an outraged Daniel Webster grimly, "that great wrong has been done to the Cherokee."

Michigan victimized the Chippewas who had been given their reservation by a U.S. treaty signed in 1854. In 1869 speculators discovered valuable minerals on their lands. Successfully lobbying the Michigan legislature to put these areas up for sale, they made fortunes by grabbing them for a pittance.

Washington and Main Street saw mutual advantage in decimating the Indians and seizing their lands.

"First there was military assault, on slight pretexts or no pretexts at all," observed John Collier, appointed by FDR to head the Bureau of Indian Affairs in 1933, ". . . [then] annihilation, with the United States Army as the driving power. The tribes were finally beaten . . . through starvation after the whites had destroyed the buffalo. . . . That revelry of slaughter . . . was recognized as a war measure against the Indians and was deliberately encouraged."

Collier reversed the former BIA policy of trying to wipe out the Indian culture and make Indians over into second-class whites. He encouraged the preservation of tribal cultures, helped Indians manage their own affairs locally and provided training for life both on or off the reservation. In 1934 Congress passed the Indian Reorganization Act, under which a measure of Indian self-government began.

Although all Indians were made citizens in 1924, seven states were still using discriminatory laws to bar them from voting by 1940. It took another eight years before 100,000 Indians in Arizona and New Mexico won court orders compelling those states to recognize their voting rights.

In 1953 Congress passed a New Indian Policy resolution to prepare tribes for increasing self-government under state and local authority, with fewer controls by the BIA. But the persistence of broad dissatisfaction was made manifest by Indian sit-ins at Alcatraz and Washington, D.C., climaxed by the bitter revolt at Wounded Knee.

At one time or another, most minorities have felt the sting of injustice at the hands of Washington or Main Street, or both. The Mormons of early Utah were persecuted by the Federal government for their religious practice of polygamy. California passed discriminatory laws against the Japanese; and after Pearl Harbor the Federal government forced both Japanese residents and their American-born children (Nisei) out of their coastal homes into inland concentration camps. Mexicans and Chicanos were severely discriminated against by California, Texas, New Mexico and Arizona.

The most important struggle waged for justice by a minority has, of course, been that of black Americans. Before the Civil War, Washington was most often their enemy and Main Street

During World War II Japanese residents of California and their American-born children were forced to leave their homes for concentration camps.
(CULVER PICTURES, INC.)

(North) their ally. After Appomattox, the Federal government was usually their ally and Main Street (South) their foe.

In 1850, at southern bidding, Congress passed the coercive second Fugitive Slave Act compelling citizens of any state, under orders, to help recapture runaway slaves. Those who refused or hindered recapture could be fined or jailed.

"By God, I will not obey it!" vowed Ralph Waldo Emerson. Citizens in every northern state joined him in obstructing enforcement of the Act and in attempts to rescue slaves from the clutches of slave-catchers. In 1855 Wisconsin defied Federal authority by declaring the Act unconstitutional and therefore invalid in Wisconsin. An elaborate Underground Railroad was developed throughout the North to help runaway slaves escape to Canada.

The Dred Scott decision burst with dramatic impact upon the nation. When this Missouri slave sued for his freedom on grounds

Dred Scott's petition for
freedom polarized the
nation in 1857.
(THE BETTMANN ARCHIVE, INC.)

that he had lost his slave status by being taken to the free state of
Illinois and the free territory of Minnesota, the Supreme Court
ruled in 1857 that, because of slave ancestry, he was not a citizen
of either Missouri or the United States, and therefore ineligible to
sue in a Federal court. The Scott case polarized the nation
irreconcilably.

Stephen Douglas, running against Lincoln for the Senate,
urged that Main Street be the final arbiter of slavery: "The
remedy is to banish the slavery question from the Halls of
Congress; remand it to the people of the territories and of the
states. . . . If the people of a territory want slavery, they have a
right to have it, and if they do not want it, no power on earth
should force it upon them. . . . In the hot climate where the
people cannot work in the open sun, where rice, the cotton plant,
and sugarcane flourish, you must have negro slaves to work there
or you must abandon the country to the crocodile."

When Lincoln entered the White House, he conceded that
Federal power should not infringe upon states' rights to slavery.
Even his famous Emancipation Proclamation of 1863 did not set

all slaves free, but was intended as a political weapon to cripple the Confederate states by setting *their* slaves free. Secretary of State William Seward scoffed at the Proclamation as "emancipating slaves where we cannot reach them, and holding them in bondage where we can set them free."

When zealous General John Frémont ordered the slaves of Unionist Missouri set free, Lincoln fired him.

After the Union's victory and Lincoln's assassination, a schism developed in Washington between the Radical Republicans controlling Congress, who were determined to enforce black equality in the southern states, and President Andrew Johnson, who objected to keeping the South under military rule.

In 1865 Congress set up the Freedman's Bureau under the War Department for the care and protection of freed slaves. The Bureau found itself frustrated by Black Codes passed by southern legislatures giving limited rights to blacks, but withholding others on various pretexts. In April 1866 Congress then passed a Civil Rights Act conferring U.S. citizenship on freed blacks, and making it a Federal misdemeanor to violate their rights. Johnson vetoed the bill.

"In the exercise of State policy over matters exclusively affecting the people of each State," he insisted, "it has frequently been thought expedient to discriminate between the two races." He branded the Act another step toward "concentration of all legislative powers in the national Government."

Congress angrily passed the bill over his veto. And to make sure that the Supreme Court could not undo the Act, two months later it also passed the Fourteenth Amendment. The Radicals then set about clamping tighter controls on the southern states with a series of four Reconstruction Acts.

The first divided the South into five military districts and protected the rights of black freedmen with Federal bayonets. Another Act compelled each former rebel state to call a constitutional convention ratifying the Fourteenth Amendment and guaranteeing black suffrage. Although Johnson vetoed the Reconstruction Acts, their passage over his veto compelled him to enforce them. Mississippi tried to stop him, but in 1867 the Supreme Court held the President beyond the reach of judicial restraint in the exercise of his powers (*State of Mississippi v. Johnson*).

A split in northern ranks between Radical and moderate Republicans let southern whites regain political control of their states. Public opinion in the North gradually turned against the effort and expense of trying to impose a new social order on the South. The Supreme Court's 1873 ruling in the *Slaughterhouse Cases*, holding that the great body of civil rights fell under the protection of the states, was the beginning of the end of the Reconstruction period.

In one final halfhearted effort to stop the erosion, the Radicals managed to pass the Civil Rights Act of 1875, prohibiting discrimination in public places and subjecting violators to Federal prosecution. But the Supreme Court declared it unconstitutional in 1883 on grounds that the Fourteenth Amendment prohibited discriminatory actions only by states, not by private individuals or companies. "The South is determined that come what may she must control the social relations of the two races," declared *Atlanta Constitution* editor Henry W. Grady. He added, "It is right that she should have this control."

When a Louisiana law segregated the state's public carriers, the Supreme Court felt compelled to overturn it in 1878 because interstate commerce was under Washington's authority (*Hall v. De Cuir*). But in 1896 the Court ruled that Louisiana was not discriminating as long as it provided "separate but equal" railroad cars. *Plessy v. Ferguson* gave southern states the right to maintain and enforce a caste society.

The Court was ambivalent about black justice before the bars of southern states. In West Virginia one black brought criminal charges against a magistrate for enforcing a state law barring blacks from jury service. The Supreme Court upheld the charges in 1880, striking down the state law as unconstitutional (*Strauder v. West Virginia*). But during the same term the Court also ruled that an accused black convicted by an all-white jury had to prove that blacks had been excluded from the jury *deliberately* (*Virginia v. Rives*).

By the end of the nineteenth century, Jim Crow laws had effectively made dead letters of the Fourteenth and Fifteenth Amendments in southern states. Black resistance was crushed by over 2,000 verified lynchings in the last two decades alone.

Blacks looked hopefully once more to Washington when a liberal Democratic administration won the White House in 1912.

The Ku Klux Klan continued to demonstrate its power as late as 1939.
(WIDE WORLD PHOTOS)

But once elected, Virginia-born Woodrow Wilson instituted segregation in Government bureaus and the District of Columbia, as well as in military units formed during World War I.

Service in that war made black veterans feel that they had earned the right to unsegregated travel, job, housing and voting opportunities. Clashes with resistant whites in 1919 led to twenty-five race riots throughout the country. The Department of Justice, called upon for Federal action to protect civil rights, replied that murder and lynching were state problems.

The race riots led to renewed growth and activity for the Ku Klux Klan, which spread through the North as well as the South. By 1925 there were some five million Klansmen in America, powerful enough to control legislatures in Colorado, Texas, Oklahoma, Louisiana, Maine and Kansas. "We are afraid of competition with peoples who would destroy our standard of living," admitted Imperial Wizard Hiram W. Evans in 1926.

Scandals involving Klan leaders, and a whopping tax fine by the Internal Revenue Service, put the Klan out of business soon after the outbreak of World War II.

In 1938 northern senators tried to pass an Anti-Lynching Bill, but were beaten by a southern filibuster that labeled it an unconstitutional invasion of state sovereignty. The Roosevelt administration then created a Civil Rights Section in the Justice Department to enforce the constitutional rights of blacks in the South.

The Truman administration, feuding with the southern states, challenged their doctrine of White Supremacy. In July 1948 Truman ordered "equality of treatment of all persons in the Armed Services without regard to race, color, religion, or national origin." He also asked Congress for a new Civil Rights Act that would abolish state and local poll taxes; end segregation in interstate travel; and make lynching a Federal offense.

The South was appalled. Senator James Eastland of Mississippi took the lead in demanding a bolt from the Democratic Party to oppose Truman's bid for reelection. Senator Harry Byrd of Virginia threatened "bloodshed" in the South if the Civil Rights Act were passed. When Truman refused to back down, 6,000 outraged southern delegates met in convention at Birmingham under the banner of the National States' Rights Party, nominating South Carolina Governor J. Strom Thurmond as their candidate for President.

"There are not enough troops in the Army," warned Thurmond, "to break down segregation and admit the Negro into our homes, our eating places, our swimming pools, and our theaters." Reporters observed that Truman was simply pursuing policies advocated by Roosevelt. "I agree," Thurmond replied testily, "but Truman really *means* it!" Truman's election victory did not dampen the determination of southern segregationists to resist all Federal civil rights programs.

During the 1950–60 decade over a million and a half blacks left the southern states to seek a better life in the North. Huge numbers, poorly educated and untrained by the South, ended up on the welfare rolls of northern states.

The arrest of Mrs. Rosa Parks in Montgomery, Alabama, for refusing to relinquish her seat on a bus to a white man led to the bus boycott that lasted a full year. In 1956 the Supreme Court

Rosa Parks arrives at the Montgomery courthouse to be arraigned for participating in the bus boycott which began when she refused to yield her seat to a white man.

(WIDE WORLD PHOTOS)

ruled that segregated seating on municipal busses violated the Constitution (*Gayle v. Browder*).

President Dwight D. Eisenhower grew increasingly disturbed by the intimidation of blacks in southern states when they sought to exercise their right to register and vote. "In Georgia, South Carolina, and Florida," he noted, "the FBI was not permitted to interview a prisoner complaining of a civil rights violation without the presence of a prison official—in South Carolina, without the written permission of the governor himself." He determined to assure blacks the right to vote because then "the American Negro could use it to help secure his other rights."

The 1957 Civil Rights Act was the first such Federal legislation since 1875. It authorized the Attorney General to initiate civil court actions to enforce the right to vote. The enforcement provision was weak, however, because of compromises forced by southern senators' threat of a filibuster.

Between 1960 and 1966 when black defendants in southern civil rights cases appealed local court decisions against them, their appeals were rejected by the appellate courts of eleven southern states in three out of four cases. But when they appealed further to the U.S. Supreme Court, they won reversals in ninety-four per cent of the cases. There was no question in the minds of southern blacks as to whether they could expect a fairer brand of justice from Washington or Main Street.

In 1960 a new Civil Rights Act further strengthened the power of the Federal government to enforce black suffrage in the South by permitting the Federal registration of voters denied state or local registration on some pretext. Segregationists, infuriated by what they regarded as a Federal assault on states' rights, retaliated with a campaign of violence, bombing and burning black people's churches, schools and homes.

Southern police began arresting civil rights demonstrators on pretexts of "impeding traffic" and "endangering the public safety by inflammatory slogans and speeches." The U.S. Supreme Court threw out such convictions as obvious infringements of the First and Fourteenth Amendments (*Thompson v. City of Louisville*, 1960; *Garner v. Louisiana*, 1961).

The Supreme Court of Georgia upheld the conviction of six blacks, who had played basketball in a customarily restricted public park, for "unlawful assembly and disturbing the peace." But in 1961 the U.S. Supreme Court reversed the conviction as enforcing racial segregation (*Wright v. Georgia*).

When 200 black students walked to the statehouse grounds in Columbia, S. Carolina, to protest discriminatory laws and actions, they were arrested for "breach of peace and trespass." The state Supreme Court upheld their convictions. But the U.S. Supreme Court ruled that the Fourteenth Amendment "does not permit a State to make criminal the peaceful expression of unpopular views" (*Edwards v. South Carolina*, 1963).

Under Georgia law persons charged with "insurrection" were not entitled to bail. A Sumter County prosecutor sought to use that law to drive SNCC civil rights organizers out of the state. Charging them with "insurrection," he threw them in jail for three months and refused to let their cases come before the grand jury until they promised to stop organizing or to leave Georgia immediately. On appeal a Federal district court declared the insurrection statute unconstitutional and issued an injunction preventing the prosecutor from persecuting the defendants for exercising civil rights (*Aelony v. Pace*, 1963).

Virginia sought to enforce a 1956 state law prohibiting anyone not directly involved in a case from soliciting legal business. The NAACP and its legal counsel were convicted for having aided blacks in litigation. The Supreme Court overturned the verdict, holding that the NAACP's litigation was "a form of political expression," and that the Virginia law could "easily become a weapon of oppression" (*NAACP v. Button*, 1963).

An important test of the rights of sit-in demonstrators came when a group of blacks in New Orleans were arrested in McCrory's chain store for demanding service at the lunch counter reserved for whites only and refusing to leave when the manager so ordered. They were arrested and convicted under a "criminal mischief" statute. The Louisiana Supreme Court upheld the conviction on grounds that the store manager—not the city or state—had brought about the arrest and charges. American law, said the court, protected the owner of private property against any trespassers.

But the U.S. Supreme Court struck down the convictions in 1963. Chief Justice Warren noted that a week before the arrests, the New Orleans Chief of Police had warned sitters-in at Woolworth's, "The police department and its personnel is ready and able to enforce the laws of the city of New Orleans and Louisiana." It was the "voice of the state" that had brought about the arrests, not merely the chain store manager. Justice Douglas added that, in any event, "When the doors of a business are open to the public, they must be open to all regardless of race" (*Lombard v. Louisiana*).

Senator Jacob Javits of New York pointed out in 1963 that in the cities of fifteen southern and border states, segregation was still practiced by sixty-five per cent of all hotels and motels, and by sixty per cent of all restaurants and theaters. Of cities and towns under 10,000 population, eighty-five to ninety per cent practiced segregation. These restrictions affected not only blacks living in the South but also all traveling through it.

Soaring black unrest led to President Lyndon B. Johnson's comprehensive Civil Rights Act of 1964. Designed to take the civil rights movement "out of the streets," it sharply defined and outlawed discrimination in eleven provisions. The bill represented a final attempt by Congress to compel southern states to obey the spirit and letter of the Fourteenth Amendment.

Forbidding discrimination in public places, the new Act

In the late 1960s the cry for black power arose in northern cities.
(CLAUS C. MEYER, BLACK STAR)

empowered the Attorney General to sue for school desegregation; set up an Equal Employment Opportunity Commission; guaranteed the right to vote; and authorized the withholding of Federal funds from any community spending them unfairly.

Echoing Andrew Jackson in the Marshall decision invalidating Georgia's anti-Indian laws, Alabama Governor George Wallace snapped, "The liberal left-wingers have passed it. Now let them employ some pinknik social engineers in Washington to figure out what to do with it!"

The South was swift to test the constitutionality of the new Civil Rights Act. The Georgia Supreme Court upheld the right of an Atlanta motel located near major highways to bar blacks. But Justice Tom Clark ruled for the U.S. Supreme Court that the Act was constitutional in banning such discrimination because of a "harmful effect" on interstate commerce (*Heart of Atlanta Motel, Inc. v. United States,* 1964).

In 1965 the widely held belief that civil rights were only a problem in southern states was exploded by the riots in Watts, the ghetto of Los Angeles. If discrimination was open and blunt in the South, it was indirect but nonetheless real in the North and West. The cry for "Black Power" was now heard in northern cities among black leaders who demanded open housing laws to let black families break out of the ghettos.

Their expectations aroused by so many Federal laws and Supreme Court decisions in their favor, many blacks grew impatient and disillusioned with the molasses-like progress toward real equality in their daily lives. Black rioting and firebombing broke out in northern cities. Southern segregationists were not unhappy to see the northern states "getting a taste of their own medicine." White northern support for civil rights causes fell off sharply, affecting Congress.

There was no enthusiasm for a new Civil Rights Act in 1966, and it failed to pass. The Supreme Court itself seemed to be having second thoughts that year when Justice Black wrote the majority opinion upholding the conviction of black civil rights workers in Florida for invading state-held property.

When a new Civil Rights Act was finally passed in 1968, it provided for the gradual elimination of discrimination in housing and made it a Federal crime to intimidate or injure anyone exercising civil rights. But southern congressmen succeeded in tacking on an antiriot provision, making it also a Federal offense to cross state lines to start or further a riot, or to give aid to any rioters.

"We have the leaders of SNCC and similar organizations going around from state to state preaching Black Power and inciting riots," complained Mississippi Congressman William Colmer. "Here we are with one Stokely Carmichael and one Rap Brown . . . traveling from state to state and from city to city, and in their wake comes conflagration, blood-spilling, wholesale pilfering and the loss of life and property."

Attorney General Ramsey Clark vainly opposed the Anti-Riot Act, insisting that riots were the constitutional responsibility of states and localities. "Government has an absolute duty to do what it can to enlarge the opportunities of the people to speak," he pointed out, "and a bill like this does just the opposite. It makes it exceedingly dangerous."

The Nixon administration won two terms with the help of a

"Southern strategy" that privately promised southern leaders it would be slow to enforce civil rights laws. The President opposed bussing as a means of school integration, and sought to kill the Office of Economic Opportunity (OEO) set up to provide vocational training and jobs for the ghettos. Four members of the U.S. Civil Rights Commission resigned in protest.

In March 1973 blacks and Chicanos joined in storming Los Angeles City Hall, denouncing the city council for plans that would chop funds for their Model Cities program in half.

"You're yelling at the wrong people," a councilman told them. The real trouble, he explained, was that the Nixon administration had cut off Federal funds for the project. Model Cities administrator Rolland J. Curtis advised the demonstrators, "Go to Washington and raise hell."

State after state, city after city, discovered that the Nixon administration's "revenue-sharing" program did not compensate for the shutting down of important Federal programs for minorities. Most states preferred to use the Washington funds they received to benefit home majorities instead. The minorities quickly recognized that they could hope for small comfort or aid from state legislatures.

"In viewing the incidence of affronts to civil rights in this country," observed Ohio State University political scientist Lawrence J. R. Herson, "it is difficult not to conclude that the traditional enemy of these rights has been, not the Federal government, but the states."

Minorities have become disillusioned with the fruits of the efforts made by Washington to give them full equality with other citizens. They are cynical about what they can expect from Main Street. More and more they have become determined to get their rights by winning control of ghetto schools, businesses, welfare programs, police, courts and elective offices, and solving their problems by exercising their own powers.

9 · *Who must help the cities?*

*I*n *New York City Puerto Rican mother with two* small children is awakened by the scream of her two-year-old daughter. Leaping out of bed, she seizes a hammer and races to the crib. An animal almost the size of a small cat springs out over the slats, and dashes to safety through a hole in the wall. There is blood on the ear of the crying baby where the huge rat has sunk its teeth.

It is 1967. In the White House President Lyndon B. Johnson is preparing to send Congress a bill providing $10 million in Federal grants to local neighborhoods, for developing and carrying out rat control and extermination efforts.

"Every year," he reports, "thousands of people, especially those living in the slums of our cities, are bitten by rats in their homes and tenements. The overwhelming majority of victims are babies lying in their cribs. Some of them die of their wounds. Many are disfigured for life."

The Rat Extermination and Control Act comes up for a vote in the House of Representatives in July. Conservative Republicans and Democrats join forces to kill the bill by ridicule. Congressman Joel Broyhill of Virginia chuckles, "Mr. Speaker, I think the 'rat smart thing' for us to do is to vote down this rat bill 'rat now.'" Other congressmen joke about appointing a High Commissioner of Rats; "throwing money down a rathole"; a new

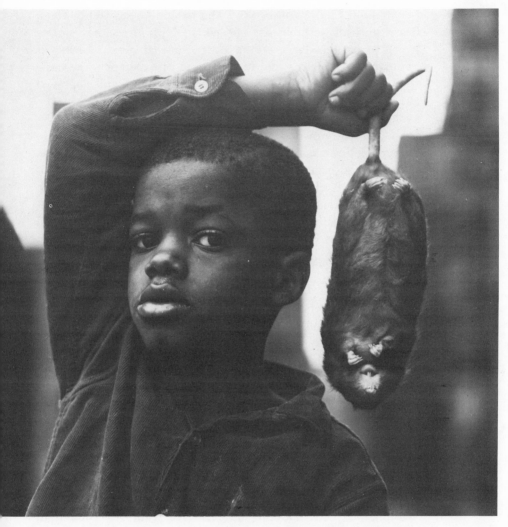

A young citizen of New York City displays the target of the Extermination and Control Act of 1967.

"civil rats bill"; and "discriminating between city and country rats." The House rocks with laughter.

The bill is voted down 207 to 176.

"When I heard the description of this sorry spectacle," the President declares, "I felt outraged and ashamed."

Deploring the predicament of the modern city, New York

Mayor John Lindsay observed, "The federal government, which has historically established our national priorities, has simply never really thought that the American city was 'worthy' of improvement—at least not to the extent of expending any basic resources on it. As a center of unhealthy, immoral and depraved citizens, the city has seemed to many . . . a condition to be avoided, not a problem to be solved."

So our overcrowded cities have been left to decay despite billions in Federal revenues collected from city taxpayers. The states have also shown little inclination to help. Whose responsibility is it, actually, to aid the cities?

Many Americans do not think that Washington ought to get involved in Main Street's programs. ("Taxes collected from all should be spent for the benefit of all, not on a few." "Let each city and community take care of its own problems." "Why should *my* hard-earned money be taxed to support all those city loafers on welfare?")

There is also opposition because Federal urban aid often results in an expensive bureaucracy being set up to oversee the operation of a program, with red tape and endless delays. Some critics charge that Washington's grants-in-aid are bribes to induce state and city support for Federal programs.

The Indiana General Assembly adopted a defiant resolution in the 1950s: "We have decided that there is no such thing as 'Federal' aid. We know that there is no wealth to tax that is not already within the boundaries of the 48 states. So we propose henceforward to tax ourselves and take care of ourselves. We are fed up with subsidies, doles and paternalism. We are no one's stepchild. We have grown up. We serve notice that we will resist Washington, D.C. adopting us. . . . We want government to come home."

But in the subsequent five years, Federal aid to both state and local governments more than doubled for hospital construction, low-rent housing and job training. Federal grants for public health, highways, slum clearance and urban renewal increased by as much as 500 per cent. Fiercely independent Indiana joined the rest of the states in accepting this aid.

Advocates of Federal aid argue that without it, some states can't afford to take care of their needy and underprivileged, while others just won't spend the money. Moreover, many cities are practically at war with rural-controlled state legislatures and can't get essential funds from the state capital. As a result the needy are often forced to move to more humane states, penalizing those states with an added welfare burden.

In 1923 the state of Massachusetts asked the courts to declare illegal the Shepard-Towner Act, which provided Federal grants-in-aid for promoting maternal and infant health and welfare. The state charged that the grants constituted Federal interference in state affairs. The Supreme Court ruled the Act constitutional (*Massachusetts v. Mellon*). Since then grants-in-aid have been dispensed by Washington to assist all kinds of governmental programs at lower levels.

The New Deal unleashed a torrent of direct financial aid to cities impoverished by the Depression. Almost all of the nation's cities turned Democratic in gratitude, especially since this "pump-priming" process helped get the economy moving.

The cities fell into serious trouble once more following World War II, when blacks surged up from the South to crowd the northern ghettos. Millions of white city dwellers were aided in their flight to the suburbs by the Federal Housing Administration's low-interest mortgages. A $60 billion National Defense Highways program also built parkways between the suburbs and the inner city, making it possible to commute to work.

Deserted by millions of middle-class whites, the cities were left helpless because the millions of jobless blacks and Puerto Ricans who replaced them often had to be fed, clothed and housed at public expense. The cities had nowhere to turn but to the Federal government, because rural-dominated legislatures were invariably deaf to their pleas for help.

"A basic issue in almost every state legislature—and indeed in the politics at large of almost every state—is the conflict between town and country," noted journalist John Gunther. "The distrust of big cities by rural areas is a factor in American history almost as old as the history itself."

From 1950 to 1965 Federally supported programs for both the cities and states multiplied until they were costing $20 billion annually. Grants-in-aid were provided for transportation, water purification, pollution control, schools, hospitals, parks, flood control, beach erosion, urban renewal and planning, housing,

Federal grants sustained the quality of suburban life, while the cities decayed.

(CAROL BASEN)

business loans, power plants and public buildings. Washington reserved the right to set standards for such programs, to approve or disapprove state and local plans and to inspect the projects for fidelity to blueprints.

State legislatures were often unenthusiastic about providing matching funds for Federal grants-in-aid to the cities.

"Rural areas have been so successful in focusing national attention on the farm problem," Philadelphia Mayor Richardson Dilworth told an American Municipal Association convention in 1958, "that our government spends more money annually on potatoes than it does on renewal of the great metropolitan areas in which 70 per cent of our people live."

He warned, "Unless the city problem is raised to the same level of national consciousness and effective steps are taken to halt the steady erosion of our cities, our nation faces a damaging loss in national strength almost as great as that which could be inflicted by enemy action."

During the Eisenhower years, Federal grants aided schools in suburban and rural areas far more than city schools. They built intrastate highways but not badly needed city mass transportation. In 1960 the minorities in the cities turned out to vote strongly for John F. Kennedy, who promised them a fairer distribution of Federal funds for city schools, mass transit, welfare programs, low-cost housing and pollution control.

After his election Kennedy sought to make state legislatures more responsive to the cities by pressing for reapportionment, to give cities a fairer representation of state legislators. Rural politicians controlling state legislatures fought delaying actions against this redistribution of power.

Kennedy also stepped up grant-in-aid payments in 1962, so that in relatively poor states like Alabama, Alaska, Arkansas, South Dakota, Vermont and Wyoming, the funds provided over twenty-four per cent of all state and local revenues.

After Kennedy's assassination, President Johnson announced his "War on Poverty," with the Economic Opportunity Act of 1964 as its cornerstone. Local political bosses were incensed when OEO undercut their patronage powers by offering minority groups a direct "piece of the action"—the opportunity to participate in local administration of OEO programs. In Chicago, Mayor Richard Daley maintained a tight grip on the antipoverty program operating in that city, spurning any Federal grants that bypassed his political machine.

Some mayors were apprehensive about cooperating with OEO because of doubts about how long Washington could be depended upon to remain a partner. "I knew that once Nixon won," said Mayor Kevin White of Boston, "I would be asked to pick up whatever programs he succeeded in tossing out."

In some southern cities the antipoverty program was found helpful in avoiding riots and winning racial peace. OEO also provided jobs for many of the minority poor who had been in jail and couldn't get any other jobs on the city payroll.

It was rare for any governor to put pressure on a state legislature to provide aid for the cities. This happened in New York State, however, where Governor Nelson Rockefeller in 1968 threatened to withhold personal favors, such as patronage, from legislators if they did not reverse their vote against a $6 billion urban slum clearance program. When another vote was taken, the legislature complied with the Governor's wishes.

In 1966 President Johnson won passage of the Model Cities Act, which he called "one of the major breakthroughs of the 1960s." Providing block grants of Federal funds to sixty-three cities for a coordinated attack on the social and physical causes of urban blight, it compelled the cities to plan and develop their own reconstruction. "This legislation," the President said, "provided a graphic test of the federal government's ability to work in harmony with other levels of government."

In New York, Mayor John Lindsay was enthusiastic: "This kind of control, in which the federal government supervises the performance of activities it helps to finance without dictating the procedures of such activities, will . . . accelerate the improvement of those neighborhoods in real need of help."

He explained, "Most of the key decisions—in terms of development, recreation, sanitation, housing, and jobs—are made not by federal officials but by the neighborhood itself through an elected council. . . . The federal government retains enough control—as it must—to check against both a misuse of funds and improper delivery of necessary services."

This new style of Federal aid bypassed the state legislatures and, therefore, much of the red tape and anticity hostility that had crippled previous aid programs. "Already vast federal sums for city improvement and rehabilitation flow directly from Washington to the cities," Maryland Senator Joseph D. Tydings noted approvingly in 1967, "without touching base in the Governor's mansion or state house. This trend is likely to continue unless the states become more meaningful partners."

There was some hope that this might happen by the end of 1966, when every state legislature had finally been reapportioned according to the "one-man, one-vote" principle ordered by the Supreme Court. For the first time in American history, the legislators elected in each state represented approximately equal numbers of people, giving the cities a more equitable voice in voting for bills they desperately needed.

But in many states the anticity vote still remained a majority. One reason was the hostility of the newly populous suburbs. "Reapportionment has suburbanized the legislatures," complained Mayor Wes Uhlman of Seattle, "and the suburbanites are as hostile to the city as the farmers ever were." The New York Times noted in 1970 that "in state after state, rising suburban strength has meant rising opposition to legislation benefiting cities."

In Missouri, at the 1969 session of the state legislature, a bill to give greater freedom to local governments was passed by the House and approved by a Senate committee. But somehow the bill was never voted upon before adjournment, and Missouri's decaying cities were left without power to raise badly needed revenues for another year and a half.

Critics of direct Federal-to-city aid object that, without the controlling hand of the state, much funding is lost through corruption and inefficiency. New York City Councilman Robert Postel charged that from 1969 to 1972 the city had lost or wasted $2.7 billion through corruption, mismanagement or neglect. He insisted that $32 million had been lost in 1969 because the city's Housing Authority chairman simply forgot to apply for Federal and state housing funds, while another $60 million had been lost in a municipal loan program to unscrupulous real estate speculators, who failed to rehabilitate the slum buildings they were paid to make livable.

The two terms of the Nixon administration swung the pendulum sharply away from Kennedy-Johnson Federalism. National expenditures were slashed to the point that led Pat Moynihan, the President's adviser on urban affairs, to warn that Federal grants-in-aid would have to be doubled if any progress was to be made in urban employment, housing and education.

In a nationally televised speech in 1969, President Nixon described his concept of a "New Federalism" to the National Governors Conference. He promised "power, funds and authority . . . increasingly to those governments closest to the people . . . returning a greater share of control to state and local authorities. . . . Washington . . . will refrain from telling states and localities how to conduct their affairs."

Instead of making grants-in-aid for special Federal programs, the President explained, revenue-sharing would provide funds directly to local authorities, who could use them to solve their own problems in their own way.

Because Democrats held political power in most cities, however, direct antipoverty funds were given instead to the states, which were not inclined to hand the money over to the cities. The total amount of aid received by the cities proved far less than they had received under previous administrations.

"Cities are broke," complained John J. Gunther, executive director of the U.S. Conference of Mayors. Newark Mayor Hugh Addonizio declared, "We have a $1 billion blueprint, but where are we going to get the $1 billion?"

Over 115 Federal programs were killed under the New Federalism. In 1973 Congresswoman Barbara Jordan of Texas charged that the Nixon budget reflected "an incredible and callous indifference to the real human needs of the people." Federal programs of health, education and welfare for the poor, the young, the aged, the blind and handicapped were among those either seriously cut back or wiped out.

Meanwhile the cities were groaning under the burden of soaring welfare costs. "The cities cannot wait for a reluctant Washington to act," John Lindsay warned Albany. ". . . New York State should relieve all the cities and counties of the state of the cost of welfare." In the long run, he prophesied, Washington would have to assume the full costs of an improved system. The reason? "No one else can."

The question of who must help the cities, and how, is likely to be answered differently by Democratic and Republican administrations as they succeed each other in the White House. Their differences go back to the original clash between Hamiltonians and Jeffersonians. Today's Republicans hold the views of the Jeffersonians that the less Federal involvement in local problems, the better. The Democrats agree with Hamilton that only strong Federal action can solve major problems.

In 1969 Lindsay pointed out that three out of four Americans now live in the cities. "To say, then, that the problems of the cities are not the responsibility of the Federal government," he declared, "is to say that the life of most Americans is not the Federal government's concern."

On the other hand, most Republican leaders believe that democracy works best with the least amount of Federal intervention and the greatest amount of self-rule and self-help at the lowest levels of government. They also believe that vast Federal expenditures for city programs only fuel the rising spiral of inflation, because the country cannot afford them.

What we are likely to see is a compromise by both sides—a return of many Federal antipoverty, health and education programs of one kind or another, with grants-in-aid directly to the cities under Federal supervision, but with greater community planning, direction and participation.

The Federal supervisory role might be supplanted by that of the state, at such time as more state legislatures begin to show themselves truly responsive to the grave problems of our decaying cities.

10 · Rivers, roads and rails

*I*t is August 1965 and there is restless frustration among Los Angeles teen-agers in the Watts ghetto. Thousands are out of school and jobless because there are no jobs to be had in Watts. They can't afford cars to get them outside the ghetto where jobs can be found. To get around sprawling Los Angeles by bus often requires two or three transfers and long waits between busses. There is no other transportation system.

Their bitterness finds an excuse to erupt in a riot that starts over the arrest of a black man charged with drunken driving. They run through the district smashing store windows, looting, setting fire to buildings and shouting, "Burn, baby, burn!" One teen-ager tells a reporter grimly, "You jus' take an' run, man; you burn when they ain't nothin' to take. You burn whitey, man. You burn his tail up so he knows what it's all about."

Before the riot is over, thirty-six are killed, 900 injured and over 4,000 are arrested. The property damage in Watts is estimated at $200 million, which would have gone a long way toward paying for an adequate transportation system needed by ghetto residents to find and hold jobs and improve their lives.

In our first years as a nation, the Federal government left it up to Main Street to look after its own development of transportation, chiefly through state turnpikes, canals and bridges. But in response to a rising nationalism, Congress voted in 1802 to give

116 ·

Soldiers of the National Guard patrol a street in Watts the day after the riot.

Federal lands to the new state of Ohio for building roads to the Ohio River.

Rapidly growing Western settlements urged the Federal government itself to undertake the building of interstate transportation systems. In 1817 young Representative John C. Calhoun of South Carolina appealed to Congress to "bind the republic together with a perfect system of roads and canals. . . . Let us conquer space." But when Congress provided Federal aid for this purpose, President James Madison vetoed the bill.

"The permanent success of the Constitution," he explained, "depends on a definite partition of powers between the General and the State Governments." His veto hit New York hardest, because that state was pushing plans for the Erie Canal. It went ahead without Federal assistance, as did Pennsylvania with its own canals and turnpikes. The result was that the chief links between the Atlantic seaboard and the West developed in the North, while the South remained isolated.

Congress tried again in 1822 by passing the Cumberland Road Act to build a Maryland turnpike. This time a veto was wielded by President James Monroe, who again held that the Constitution gave Washington no such powers.

Washington's right to control interstate transportation was tested by the invention of the steamboat by Robert Fulton. The New York legislature granted him and Robert Livingston exclusive rights of navigation on New York waters by steam-propelled vessels. They in turn licensed former New Jersey Governor Aaron Ogden to operate steamboats between both states.

But a Georgian, Thomas Gibbons, began operating a competitive steamboat line with ships licensed to engage in coastal trade by act of Congress. Ogden won a New York court injunction stopping Gibbons from operating in New York waters in violation of the state-granted monopoly. The case, a contest between state and Federal power, went to the Supreme Court.

In 1824 Justice Marshall agreed with Daniel Webster's argument for Gibbons that Congress had exclusive power over interstate commerce and that this included navigation. The High Court held that when a state and Federal law came into conflict, the state statute must give way (*Gibbons v. Ogden*).

As soon as the decision was announced, one newspaper reported, "Yesterday the steamboat *United States* . . . from New Haven, entered New York in triumph, with streamers flying, and a large company of passengers exulting in the decision of the United States Supreme Court against the New York monopoly. She fired a salute which was loudly returned by huzzas from the wharves." Popular delight was explained by the fact that within a year there were forty-three steamboats operating out of New York, with prices of tickets cut by as much as forty per cent.

Gibbons v. Ogden not only opened the way for an expansion of steam navigation in American rivers, harbors and bays but also later made possible the rapid development of a network of national railroads. The decision also encouraged fresh efforts by Congress to provide Federal aid for the development of regional transportation systems.

In 1824 Washington began giving land grants for canal projects to private companies through the state legislatures. Many canal companies were organized by unscrupulous operators who delayed the work as long as possible, then blackmailed more money out of the legislatures to complete their projects.

Federal aid for the construction of roads and canals was

nevertheless pressed enthusiastically by President John Quincy Adams. What better way to cement an expanding America together, he asked, than "by the accomplishment of works important to the whole and to which neither the authority nor the resources of any one State can be adequate?"

Congressmen who wanted Washington to pay for internal improvements in their states hit upon the method of "logrolling" ("You vote for them in my state, and I'll vote for them in yours"). When Andrew Jackson came to the White House, he tried to stop logrolling by dividing up surplus Federal funds among the states proportionately, and letting them finance their own roads and canals. He vetoed a bill for the Federal construction of a sixty-mile turnpike, the Maysville Road, within the borders of Kentucky.

"I warn you," Jackson told Congress, "against all encroachments upon the legitimate sphere of State sovereignty."

Between 1862 and 1873 Washington gave away several billion dollars' worth of public lands as grants to the railroads, to link the country by rails. Railroad magnates soon built powerful monopolies whose exorbitant and discriminatory rates, and huge profits, were protected by bribed legislators.

The Granger movement, a coalition of state farmers' associations, demanded effective state regulation of the railroads to put price ceilings on freight and passenger rates. In 1873 the Illinois State Farmers' Association resolved "that this despoilism, which defies our laws, plunders our shippers, impoverishes our people, and corrupts our government, shall be subdued and made to subserve the public interest at whatever cost."

The Illinois legislature responded by fixing maximum rates that railroad interests could charge for grain storage. When the railroads fought the law, Supreme Court Chief Justice Morrison Waite upheld it in 1877 as within a state's power to police businesses that have "a public interest."

In 1886, however, the Court struck down all state attempts to regulate interstate railroad rates, holding that this power belonged to Congress alone (*Wabash, St. Louis and Pacific Railway Company v. Illinois*). The Grange then prodded Congress into passing the Interstate Commerce Act of 1887, setting up the Interstate Commerce Commission (ICC) to control railroad rates and prevent discrimination against farmers.

The Minnesota legislature set up its own state commission with the power to fix rates within Minnesota denying the railroads any right of appeal. In 1890 the Supreme Court invalidated this act, holding that denying the railroads recourse to the courts amounted to confiscation of their property without due process of law (*Chicago, Milwaukee & St. Paul R.R. Co. v. Minnesota*).

When the People's (Populist) Party held their first national convention in Omaha in 1892, their platform declared, "We believe that the time has come when the railroad corporations will either own the people or the people must own the railroads. . . . Transportation being a means of exchange and a public necessity, the government should own and operate the railroads in the interests of the people."

The famous *Plessy v. Ferguson* case provided a test of Federal versus state power in determining operating rules for the railroads. It arose when Homer A. Plessy of Louisiana, a light-skinned black passenger, took a seat in a whites-only railroad coach and refused to move to a segregated coach. Ejected by police, he was arrested for violating state law.

Plessy challenged the right of Louisiana to provide "equal but separate" accommodations for the two races, claiming it violated his Fourteenth Amendment right to equal protection of the laws. But in 1896 Supreme Court Justice Henry B. Brown rejected "the assumption that the enforced separation of the two races stamps the colored race with a badge of inferiority." Louisiana's law, Brown said, was reasonable "with reference to the established usages, customs and traditions of the people, and with a view to the promotion of their comfort, and the preservation of the public peace and good order."

As long as laws requiring segregation did not establish unequal facilities, he added, blacks were not being denied the equal protection of the laws, even if "the colored race chooses to put that construction on it. . . . The object of the [Fourteenth] Amendment was undoubtedly to enforce the absolute equality before the law, but in the nature of things it could not have been intended to abolish distinctions based upon color, or to enforce social . . . equality."

Justice John Marshall Harlan vigorously dissented. "Our Constitution is color-blind," he insisted, "and neither knows nor tolerates classes among citizens. . . . The arbitrary separation of citizens, on the basis of race, while they are on a public highway, is a badge of servitude."

If the Court was unwilling to recognize the Fourteenth Amendment as a protector of civil rights against state discrimination in railroad travel, it was quick to apply the Amendment as a protector of railroad profits against state curbs. In 1898 it struck down a Nebraska attempt to curb high railroad rates by a state commission. The commission's rates were too low to constitute a "fair return" to the company, said the Court, thus violating the Fourteenth Amendment prohibition against confiscation of property without due process (*Smyth v. Ames*).

Bitter complaints from farm regions revealed that the Interstate Commerce Commission was not protecting farmers from being gouged by the railroads. At hearings in 1905, David Wilcox, president of the Delaware and Hudson Railroad Company, pleaded with Congressmen, "Do not be in a hurry and do not pass statutes because you think people want something done . . . for the good of the special regions which are particularly exasperated." But Congress passed the Hepburn Act of 1906, giving the ICC the power to fix fair maximum rates and compelling the railroads to go to court to prove them unfair. In five years the ICC cut over 190,000 of the prevailing rates in half.

The railroads went to court in 1913 against Minnesota because a state commission had set maximum rates for travel and freight within the state. The Supreme Court held that the state law was perfectly legal since it did not affect any interstate rates (*Minnesota Rate Cases*).

When the automobile became a major factor in transportation, Washington passed the Federal Aid Highway Act of 1916, offering states matching funds to help build state highways linking up in a national network. These subsidies mounted steadily until by 1960 they totaled almost $1 billion, financing roads that carried almost half the nation's total traffic.

When the airplane developed as a competitive method of transportation to railroads, cars and ships, Congress passed the Federal Airport Act of 1946, providing half a billion dollars of Federal grant-in-aid funds to help build a national network of airports.

Following World War II, black pressure mounted to overturn

the old *Plessy* decision. In 1946 the Supreme Court ordered an end to segregation on all railroads and busses in interstate commerce, and followed it with another decision enforcing integration in railroad dining cars.

"The threats that have been held over the South for four years," cried Georgia Governor Herman Talmadge, "are now pointed like a dagger ready to be plunged into the very heart of Southern tradition!" But the importance of mass transportation was steadily declining as Americans took to private wheels to get where they wanted to go.

By 1959 they were spending $36 billion a year on automobiles, and only $3 billion on all forms of public transport—busses, trains, subways, airplanes, taxis. States collected as much in bridge and road tolls as Americans spent on intercity bus fares. Railroads felt the pinch, cutting service and in some cases falling into bankruptcy.

Using the pretext of national defense, in 1956 Congress passed the National Defense Highways Act to launch large-scale interstate, high-speed highways linking large cities throughout the nation. The program called for spending $33 billion over thirteen years, on the basis of a ninety per cent Federal grant matched by ten per cent state grants. Responsibility for disbursing and administering these huge funds was given to state highway departments. The final cost amounted to over $60 billion.

Main Street manipulations for political purposes were part of the problem. Governor Faubus of Arkansas quietly used $3 million of his state's share of Federal highway funds to raise salaries of top state highway officials. When this came to light, he was compelled to order his officials to return the money. Rex Whitton, administrator of the U.S. Bureau of Public Roads, also protested the action of Governor Wallace of Alabama in requiring consulting engineers on Federal highway projects to hire Klansmen as agents.

The huge superhighway program pointedly ignored the need of poorer, carless Americans in the cities for mass public transportation. Instead it gave tremendous impetus to building whole new suburbs and shopping centers, hastening the decay of the inner city. While transforming America into a huge Suburbia, it also put more Americans than ever on wheels, making the automobile a serious air pollution problem.

Noise pollution also became a problem when the airlines began flying jet planes. More and more communities grew incensed at the sonic boom and harsh noises made by flights during take-off and landing. Some sought to prevent the building of airports near residential areas.

One test case arose when an angry Pennsylvania homeowner sued Allegheny County for operating Greater Pittsburgh Airport, where planes passing at low altitudes over his house were shattering his family's nerves. The county argued that under a Federal statute, airspace needed to insure safety in landing and take-off was navigable airspace belonging to the United States. The county, therefore, could not be sued.

But in 1962 Supreme Court Justice Douglas held that under the Fourteenth Amendment the county was liable for compensation by reason of such flights. It was at fault, he found, for not having bought enough private property around the airport to make its operation bearable to county residents (*Griggs v. Allegheny County*). Justice Black dissented, holding that Washington should also pay part of the damages since the flights were not for the exclusive benefit of county residents, but were part of a national airways system.

The *Griggs* decision alarmed other counties with airports where homeowners living under jet-flight patterns began filing suits. Another key decision came in 1973 when the Supreme Court had to decide whether a citizens' group of Burbank, California, had the right to stop any night jet flights in or out of the airport, because near-by families were unable to get a decent night's sleep. This time, however, the Court held that no town, country or state law could limit the hours of flights of planes traveling interstate, as such a restriction would conflict with Federal authority over national aviation.

By 1964 it was no longer possible for Congress to ignore the desperate need of the cities for help in mass transportation. "Traffic engineers point out that if everybody now coming into Manhattan . . . were to enter by private car," *Fortune* magazine pointed out, "the whole of the island . . . would have to be given over to multiple-level parking buildings. They also calculate that . . . all land areas in [the large] cities, by 1980 or so, will be needed for parking."

Congress passed the Urban Mass Transportation Act, authorizing a modest $375 million in Federal funds to help the cities develop new subway, bus and rail systems in congested areas. The program moved at a snail's pace until 1973, when the cities finally won a bill from Congress unlocking a highway trust fund derived from gas and tire taxes, and providing well over $3 billion in direct grants for urban mass transit projects.

President Nixon, unsympathetic to huge Federal expenditures, especially for the cities, moved swiftly to impound those funds. When the state of Missouri went to court to unfreeze them, the Eighth Circuit Court of Appeals held that the U.S. Department of Transportation had to comply with the intent of Congress, instead of obeying the orders of the President (*State Highway Commission of Missouri v. Volpe*, 1973).

The United States was thrown into a kind of transportation panic when an energy crisis suddenly developed at the end of 1973 and beginning of 1974. Declaring a fuel shortage, worsened by the Arab nations' cutting off Middle East oil to the United States because of American support for Israel, the President appointed an "energy czar," William Simon, to head a new Federal Energy Office.

A New England gas station copes with the fuel shortage.
(UNITED PRESS INTERNATIONAL)

Americans were urged to drive as little as possible; to use busses and trains; to organize car pools so that fewer cars had to be driven to work. Gas stations were urged to limit sales to ten gallons a customer, and to shut down from Saturday night to Monday morning, to discourage Sunday driving. States were urged to pass fifty-five-mile speed limits.

The fuel crisis had widespread repercussions. People became afraid of being stranded if they traveled. Businesses catering to tourists, skiers and travelers were seriously hurt. Many industries which depended on a full supply of gas or petroleum byproducts began laying off thousands of workers. Independent truckers, furious at price-gouging by oil companies and gas stations, and at government attempts to slow them down on the nation's throughways, staged protest demonstrations by massive blocking of highways. Car manufacturers found themselves with expensive white elephants on their hands—big cars nobody now wanted because they guzzled too much gas—and were forced to retool the industry for small-car production.

Even as these blows were felt by an America on wheels, another transportation crisis developed. Airline flights were cut back to save fuel, and many passengers turned to the railroads, now being run by Amtrak, a government-owned passenger railroad company. But seven bankrupt railroads, including the Penn Central, threatened to shut down. Congress kept them running with a $2 billion subsidy signed by Nixon in January 1974. To keep unprofitable branch lines operating, Washington was to pay seventy per cent of the costs and local governments served would pay the rest.

Senator Vance Hartke of Indiana justified this rescue of the bankrupt railroads, which serve seventeen states and haul fourteen per cent of the nation's freight, by stating that otherwise their failure would "bring this nation to its knees from Illinois to the Atlantic Ocean."

In the not-too-distant future, with or without an oil shortage, restrictions may be necessary against taking private cars into the crowded big cities, even with pooled rides. People would drive to parking areas on the outskirts, then take a rapid transit system into the heart of the city. The 1974 transportation bill clearly indicates that in the future mass transportation will have priority over highway travel.

Even though mass transit problems basically call for solutions at the state and city level, in most cases the costs are simply too enormous for any locality to bear without Federal help. Washington will probably provide increasing grants-in-aid, justifying this Federal presence on Main Street by the fact that all city transit systems are interconnected and are therefore a Federal responsibility.

11 · Homes for Americans

"Why didn't Washington leave our neighborhood alone?" bitterly asks a sixty-eight-year-old St. Louis woman whose old slum area has been demolished by the Federal Urban Renewal Program. "All of us old people lived there all our lives. We all knew one another—it was like a home town. Now it's gone, and so are all the people we knew. Now we live in a dump worse than the old place, where we don't know nobody. This is better?"

Compounding the irony, the high-rise public housing project that goes up in place of the old St. Louis slums acquires such a bad reputation, because of robbery and muggings, that over twelve per cent of the apartments go unrented in 1973. In Pruitt-Igoe, a compound of thirty-three high-rise buildings in the middle of the city's worst slum area, three fall into such disrepair that they have to be demolished after only a few years.

Sidney Spector, a Federal official involved with housing for senior citizens, tells a Senate subcommittee, "Even under ideal circumstances, relocation is a disrupting force creating an abiding sense of crisis over the loss of a home, a neighborhood, friends and a community. For the aged . . . it comes at a time when income is lowest, health problems greatest, and when emotional attachment to a home and a way of life is most intense and necessary."

A drastic solution to an Urban Renewal mistake—buildings of the Pruitt-Igoe housing project are demolished.

Washington's attempt to provide housing for the urban underprivileged, obviously, is in deep trouble.

The Federal government first became involved in housing Americans through the Homestead Act of 1862, which gave up to 160 acres of surveyed public land to any citizen, or would-be citizen, over 21 who agreed to settle on it for five years and make certain improvements. The Act was designed to encourage settlement of the West as quickly as possible.

As a reward for Union soldiers, in 1864 Congress provided a homestead bonus for those with two years' service, subject to a one-year residence. Once homesteaders had filled up the vacant spaces Washington wanted settled, however, the matter of housing was left within the purview of the cities and states until the Depression of the 1930s threatened millions of Americans with the loss of their homes.

In 1932 banks foreclosed on the unpaid mortgages of a quarter of a million families. During the first half of 1933, over 1,000 homes a day were being sold at sheriffs' sales. City and state governments stood by in helpless paralysis. A cry arose for Washington to do something quickly to rescue homeowners.

In June 1933 Congress passed a Home Owners Refinancing Act, creating the Home Owners Loan Corporation. HOLC was authorized to issue $2 billion in bonds to refinance mortgage debts. When it opened for business in Akron, a double column of eager homeowners stretched for three blocks down Main Street before 7:00 A.M. As the doors opened, 500 people surged frantically into the lobby, hoping that the loans would not run out before their turn came.

In the Oklahoma land rush of 1889 homesteaders scrambled for Indian territory opened up to settlers by the Federal government.

(THE BETTMANN ARCHIVE, INC.)

One year later the Home Owners Loan Act extended low-interest loans for the repair and maintenance of homes. During the three crucial years Washington went to the rescue of American homeowners, the HOLC helped refinance—and save—one out of every five mortgaged private dwellings in the nation.

Congress initiated a radically new idea in June 1934—a National Housing Act designed to stimulate residential construction, promote improvement in housing standards and create a sound system of home financing. It established the Federal Housing Administration (FHA) to insure and encourage loans by private lending institutions to middle-income families, for building new homes or modernizing old ones.

But new home construction was held down by Roosevelt's curious appointment as FHA head, conservative oil executive James Moffett. Also opposing a low-cost housing program proposed by Public Works Administrator Harold Ickes, Moffett claimed it would "wreck a 21-billion dollar mortgage market and undermine the nation's real estate values."

Four years later Moffett was replaced and a liberalized FHA launched a boom in home-building. Ickes, eager to get his public housing projects under way, sought to acquire land for them by exercising the claim of eminent domain—the government's right to seize needed land and pay a reasonable price for it. When a Circuit Court stopped these seizures as unconstitutional, Ickes turned for help to Senator Robert Wagner of New York, who introduced a new Federal housing bill.

In 1937 Roosevelt pushed the Wagner-Steagall Housing Act through Congress. It created the U.S. Housing Authority as a public corporation under the Department of the Interior, making available half a billion dollars in loans for the construction of low-cost housing projects. By the end of 1940, almost 350 USHA projects were under construction.

Where authorized by state laws, city officials formed local housing authorities. If their plans met Federal specifications, the Public Housing Administration lent them most of the money needed to begin local projects. Only persons with low incomes under specified limits were eligible as tenants; they had to move when their earnings went over the limits.

Not all state or city governments were delighted by this Federal attempt to help them solve their housing problems. The

Philadelphia City Hall, for example, turned down an offer of $19 million by Washington for the construction of 3,000 low-rent homes, branding such a program "socialistic."

After World War II, Washington's housing efforts shifted in focus from the urban poor to the suburban middle-class, as millions of Americans left city apartments to seek homes in the suburbs. Many mayors held the Federal government responsible for the encroaching decay of their cities.

"What helped to spur the suburban exodus?" asked Mayor John Lindsay. "It was in large part the Federal Housing Administration's all-out effort to encourage home ownership in the years following World War II, principally through low-interest mortgages . . . which brought suburban living within the range of millions of families." Federal funds for highways, linking city jobs with suburban homes, also played a part.

Lindsay complained, "Federal money is . . . far less readily available for the building of city apartments for middle- and low-income families. Somehow it is socialistic or un-American to help a poor or working family move into an apartment. . . . Yet the financing of $30,000 and $40,000 homes in suburban developments is in the best traditions of the Founding Fathers!" In thirty-one years of subsidized housing, he charged, over ten million FHA-insured homes were built in the suburbs, compared to only 800,000 apartment units in the cities.

For many cities the question became not one of whether Washington had an obligation to help Main Street house its people, but whether that help ought to go primarily to the cities or the suburbs. Washington, meanwhile, sought to placate the ghettos by making it possible for middle-class blacks to escape slum dwellings and find better living quarters.

They were being contained in the slums by restrictive covenants that prevented them from buying or renting homes in most white communities. This was the chief method used in the North to keep neighborhoods and schools segregated. In deeds of sale, real estate operators and property owners agreed not to sell or lease property to any but "members of the Caucasian race." The justification used was that blacks had lower living standards and would not keep property up to community expectations, thus driving down property values, causing whites to sell out and turning the neighborhood black.

City and state laws keeping communities white had been declared in violation of the Fourteenth Amendment by the Supreme Court in 1917 (*Harmon v. Tyler*). But the gimmick of restrictive covenants in deeds allowed property owners to circumvent this ruling. In 1926 the Supreme Court had held that these were merely private agreements and did not constitute city or state action in violation of Federal law (*Corrigan v. Buckley*).

Corrigan kept restrictions legal until 1948, when a black would-be homeowner went to court in Maryland to protest such covenants in the deeds of residential properties. In the light of the *Corrigan* ruling, the Maryland court upheld the restrictions. But on appeal, the Supreme Court decreed that no private discriminatory policies could be enforced by any state court.

Congress, acknowledging the inequity of helping to provide over ten times as many homes for suburbanites as for city dwellers, passed the National Housing Act of 1949. If its purpose was high, its performance was low. Over six million living units of public housing built during the next two decades had to be branded "substandard"—falling to pieces or lacking full plumbing. Worse, far more slum units were destroyed to build low-rent housing than were replaced by housing projects. When neighborhoods were broken up, many residents were forced to seek shelter in other, even more crowded, slums.

During a period of anti-Communist hysteria inflamed by Senator Joseph McCarthy, Congress attached a rider to the Federal Housing appropriations bill requiring every family living in a Federally aided project to sign a loyalty oath denying any connection with the Communist Party. The New York City Housing Authority alone was required to collect affidavits from 30,000 families.

An even more exasperating example of Federal bureaucracy was the requirement that each Authority director must sign one dozen copies of an affidavit each time his agency purchased kitchen appliances. Washington rejected one director's plea to be allowed to sign an original affidavit, and rubber-stamp his signature to the other eleven copies.

In the Housing Act of 1954, Congress sought to cope with the problem of what to do with displaced urban families between the time their slum was torn down and a housing project replaced it.

Construction of 80,000 housing units was authorized over the next three years, with provisions for increased mortgages, lowered down payments and extended payment periods.

Meanwhile, private rents and building costs were soaring. Middle-class families, who could neither qualify for low-cost housing nor afford high-rise private apartments, were being frozen out of the city. And the black poor still found themselves displaced by urban renewal programs.

Historian Michael W. Miles described the situation in Chicago: "The black poor was moved out of Hyde Park-Kenwood and onto a tight housing market, driving rents still higher. There was the usual lack of adequate relocation procedures, while the rents of apartments constructed in the area were prohibitive for low-income blacks."

Intense opposition to urban renewal programs mounted in the South and West, which resented heavy expenditures of public funds to benefit chiefly the black and poor of northern cities. To prevent the Democrats from passing a bill authorizing the building of another 250,000 urban living units, President Eisenhower had Republican Senator Homer Capehart of Indiana introduce an alternative administration bill calling for the expenditure of only one tenth as much money.

Senate Majority leader Lyndon B. Johnson knew that the administration had enough votes to pass its bill. But he shrewdly persuaded southern and western senators to defeat it so that they could go home and report to their constituents that they had voted against Federal housing. Afterwards he adroitly wheeled and dealed his own bigger bill into passage.

The new Federal Urban Renewal Program permitted Washington to go to the aid of a community's public and private resources to "prevent and correct urban blight and decay and to set in motion long-range, planned development." Washington paid two-thirds of the cost, Main Street one-third.

The planning was done by city agencies, which bought out blighted areas, rebuilt some buildings and leveled others to make way for new construction. By the end of 1960, Federally aided projects of housing and urban renewal were changing the face of almost 2,000 American communities.

Cities could not accept Federal aid for their urban renewal programs without state authorization. By the end of 1961 all but

Mayor John Lindsay of New York confers with Harlem leaders as bulldozers clear space for a Model Cities project.

(WIDE WORLD PHOTOS)

five states had passed such enabling laws—the exceptions being Idaho, Louisiana, South Carolina, Utah and Wyoming. The legislatures of Connecticut, Massachusetts and New York welcomed Washington's new aid so eagerly that they even authorized grants or loans to help the cities pay their share of the projects.

The Housing Act of 1961 extended residential aid to moderate income families, 100,000 additional low-income families, the elderly and college students. Communities were also helped to obtain needed water supplies and sewage systems.

Major Richardson Dilworth of Philadelphia (which had once scorned Washington's housing aid) transformed that city at a cost of billions, largely with Federal housing funds. By 1963 urban renewal projects were going forward in 702 communities of forty-two states. Nearly half were located in cities of less than 25,000 population. In all cases public hearings were first held to obtain local government approval.

Addressing the U.S. Conference of Mayors in 1964, Mayor

Richard Tucker of St. Louis, Missouri, declared that urban renewal "in its concentrated attack on slums . . . did more to expose the ugliness and squalor of the poverty-stricken among us than any other program . . . [and] made the public generally more aware of the need to provide adequate housing for the forgotten fifth of our population. . . . Urban renewal was the first Government program, at any level of government, which said if you take a family out of the slum through a publicly sponsored clearance program, you must, if possible, relocate him in standard housing."

But the Federal Urban Renewal Program was also not without severe critics. Staunch believers in free enterprise argued that it was unnecessary because local banks, businesses, realtors and civic groups could cooperate to work out their own urban development programs without Federal aid. They charged Washington with "Marxism" for interfering in the private affairs of people by redistributing wealth through housing subsidies. Federal slum clearance was also blamed for putting small merchants out of business, because most could not afford to open new shops in the new developments.

Some critics assailed Washington for uprooting people from their old neighborhoods instead of rehabilitating those neighborhoods. Because Federal regulations required entire sites to be demolished before any new homes could begin to be built on them, red tape, construction difficulties and delays left displaced residents of the razed slums with no place to go, and only promises by the city to find them new lodgings.

Other critics deplored the new public housing projects as "automatic ghetto slums with built-in crime." Many were built in slapdash fashion, with no doors on closets, insufficient play areas for children, and no places for neighbors to gather. No taverns were permitted in the plans, since they would lay Washington open to charges of endorsing drinking. Many architects also denounced the new high-rise apartment structures as aesthetic blights on the landscape.

Defenders of the Federal Urban Renewal Program replied that Washington was twisting no one's arm. The program was entirely voluntary and had been designed to help those cities that were pleading for Federal assistance because they had been unable to get help from the community or the state.

In 1965 Congress passed a new Housing Act which increased appropriations and authorized partial payment of rent for certain low-income and handicapped families in nonprofit housing. The Act also provided grants up to $1,500 each for the rehabilitation of homes in blighted areas.

Three years later Congress passed the Housing and Urban Development Act, broadening the whole program with the announcement of a ringing national goal: "A decent home and a suitable living enivronment for every American family." But once more Washington's good intentions were tattered in enactment.

"The 1968 Housing Act," charged *New York Times* urban affairs reporter John Herbers, "has brought several hundred subsidized units—but at what a price! The crooks in the central city have had a field day with it. Much of the housing is junk, built on questionable sites, fostering the old patterns of segregation, and serving the moderate income more than the very poor, with the FHA standing happily at the till handing out federal chits. . . . I often wondered why the government did not simply make direct loans for building housing rather than paying interest subsidies that are guaranteed to lenders beyond the life of much of the housing being built . . . the government could save billions that way."

It became clear by 1973 that Washington's Urban Renewal Program was anything but a glowing success. The high-rise buildings were grossly mismanaged and quickly deteriorated into modern slums ridden with muggings and robberies.

The Secretary of Housing and Urban Development (HUD) talked of resigning and recommended that all Federal housing programs be abolished as "a $100-billion mistake." The handwriting was on the wall in November 1972 when the Senate approved a new Federal housing program, only to have the bill die in the House. Its death was ensured when the suburbs and other white neighborhoods began fighting to keep low-cost housing projects from being built in their communities.

Dissatisfaction with what many critics call "vertical instant slums" may compel new directions for public housing and urban renewal in the future. Already over a dozen states now have their own programs, including provisions for mortgage assistance and loans on low- and moderate-income housing.

In January 1973 President Nixon suspended all housing

programs, declaring that the existing programs were scandal-ridden, inefficient and too costly. He announced that he planned to set up a new over-all project, Community-Development Revenue Sharing, to replace seven current housing programs, including the Federal Urban Renewal Program.

But in July U.S. District Court Judge Charles R. Richey ruled the President's suspension order illegal. The Farmers Home Administration was also ordered to resume assistance to people with low incomes, with rural home loans at interest as low as one per cent. Pointing out that Federal housing subsidies had helped 60,000 families obtain almost $2 billion in government loans, Judge Richey observed that the Nixon administration had "placed a blockade in the road to decent housing for all" by shutting off another estimated $1.2 billion in subsidies scheduled for the next six months.

In August 1973 Mayor Lindsay proposed to Congress a Community Development Act combining existing housing and community development programs into a single block grant, along the lines of Nixon's reform plan. The cities would receive $10 billion a year for three years from Washington, with greater local control of housing needs by each city. The new plan, Lindsay argued, would "end the absurd situation where a city may have ample funds for clearing families off sites but no money with which to build housing on those sites."

With high construction costs locked into an ever higher spiral of inflation, it seems doubtful that enough low-income Americans can ever obtain decent homes or apartments unless the Federal government remains involved in some degree as a financial partner in this gigantic enterprise.

Main Street, aware that it cannot possibly tackle the problem alone, hopes that Washington has learned from past mistakes and will do a better job in the future.

12 · Who helps the farmer?

*I*n 1973 Dale James, a Nebraska hog farmer, is just beginning to get his share of the soaring national income after many hard years of scraping along. He feels indignant when housewives from coast to coast organize local meat boycotts at the supermarkets, demanding a Government rollback of meat prices. Mrs. Sheri Weiler of northern Michigan denounces the farmers of America as "greedy." James worries that the Federal government will yield to the housewives' pressure.

He issues a personal challenge to Mrs. Weiler. If she will come to his farm and last just one day of tending to his hogs, he promises her a year's free supply of pork. The challenge makes fresh headlines when Mrs. Weiler accepts.

TV cameras trail her around James's farm for a whole day, sunup to sundown, as she plunges valiantly through the muck trying to do his job. By the end of the day she has won the wager, but confesses that she has never worked so hard or so long in her whole life. "Dale James," she admits, "earns every damn dime he gets." Coast-to-coast news coverage of the story helps defuse some of the housewives' anger against the farmers.

And Washington doesn't roll back meat prices.

A special relationship has always existed between American farmers and their national government. Thomas Jefferson wrote

SHAYS'S MOB IN POSSESSION OF A COURT-HOUSE.

Massachusetts farmers take possession of a courthouse in Shays' Rebellion.

in 1782, "Those who labor in the earth are the chosen people of God, if he ever had a chosen people."

The Federal government tried to increase their numbers at the conclusion of the Revolutionary War by paying off with Federal land grants the pauperized troops who were owed back pay by bankrupt states. Some veterans sold their land, but many settled on it and turned farmer.

The earliest complaints of the farmers were directed against state legislatures, many of which were controlled by East Coast merchants and bankers, for passing laws exploiting poor debtors. Farmers were often stripped of their land, cattle and possessions because of their inability to pay heavy state taxes or repay usurious loans.

Some were flung into debtors' prison. In 1786 Massachusetts was the scene of Shays' Rebellion, when mobs of farmers prevented courts from sitting so that no judgments could be passed against them. Governor James Bowdoin issued a proclamation against unlawful assemblies and called out the state militia. The poor farmers, calling themselves Regulators, elected as their leader war hero Daniel Shays, who could not pay off a $12 debt. He led 1,100 farmers in shutting down the state Supreme Court at Springfield which was preparing to indict him and other Regulator leaders for "treason."

Storming prisons, the Regulators freed jailed debtors, then sought to raid the Federal arsenal for arms. But the militia scattered them with artillery and pursued them through the countryside. Fourteen taken prisoner were sentenced to die as traitors until a storm of public protest compelled the Governor to pardon some farmers and let others off with short prison terms. Popular indignation swept the old legislature out of office, and a new one instituted reforms.

The Whisky Rebellion, discussed earlier, was another famous revolt against government oppression—this time by the Federal government. Hamilton's use of a Federalized militia to suppress the Pennsylvania whisky farmers provoked such repercussions that the Federalists lost power, with Jefferson swept into the White House as a states' rights advocate.

When farmers felt oppressed by the money monopoly of the Second Bank of the United States, they found a champion in President Andrew Jackson, who vetoed renewal of the Bank's charter for discriminating against the poor in favor of the rich. "The farmers . . . who have neither the time nor the means of securing like favors to themselves," he said, "have a right to complain of the injustice of their Government."

During the first half of the nineteenth century, most farmers continued to regard state legislatures, not Congress, as their enemy. In 1839 tenant farmers on the old feudal estates of New York rose in revolt against a gouging rent system used by manorial lords like the Schuylers, Livingstons, Van Rensselaers and Van Cortlandts. Over 100,000 tenant farmers lived in bondage to the Van Rensselaer family alone.

Staging antirent riots, they demanded an end to the feudal leasehold racket that kept most Hudson River Valley farmers in landless poverty. But the New York State legislature was in the pockets of the patroons and turned a deaf ear. Donning Indian garb, the tenant farmers went on the warpath and waged an antirent war against the patroons.

Sheriffs attempting to serve dispossess notices were met by masked men who blew tin horns to summon other "Indians," and the sheriffs were driven off violently. When the farmers' leader, Smith Boughton, was arrested, farmers on both sides of the Hudson staged a mass torchlight procession up the river toward the town of Hudson, where he was being held in prison. The mayor was warned to release Boughton, or Hudson would go up in flames. Frightened, he appealed to Governor William H. Seward for state militia, which soon appeared with flags flying, drums beating and artillery ready for action.

The farmers fled. The patroons, determined to crush the revolt, rammed antiriot laws through the New York legislature. The Governor was pressured to make mass arrests of farmers, and appoint patroon-controlled judges and prosecutors to try them. Unfair trials and harsh sentences appalled not only all of New York State, but the whole nation.

Mounting an election campaign against "Patroon law and Landlord judges," supporters of the farmers won control of the legislature. Reforms in the state constitution provided for the popular election of judges and abolished "feudal tenures of every description." But New York farmers continued to view the state as their enemy because the new reform laws were often sabotaged by officials subservient to the manor lords.

In May 1862 Congress won farmers' support for the Civil War by creating the U.S. Department of Agriculture. The Department served farmers by circulating agricultural information; conducting research in crop and livestock production, farm management, pest control, soil and water conservation; providing crop reports; offering market services; eradicating animal diseases; administering laws to protect farmers, including price support programs; and making loans to farmers.

In 1862 Congress also passed the Morrill Act transferring to each state loyal to the Union cause 30,000 Federal acres for every senator and representative in Congress. The land and sales proceeds from the surplus were used to build sixty-nine land-grant colleges to serve Middle and Far West farmers.

Following the Civil War, farmers fell upon hard times as a result of the overexpansion of agriculture, declining farm prices, extortionist railroad freight rates, and usurious bank interest rates on loans and mortgages. A Nebraska farm editor complained in 1870, "We have three crops—corn, freight rates and interest. One is produced by the farmers who farm the land by toil and sweat. The other two are produced by men who sit in their offices . . . and farm the farmers."

The Grange, founded in 1867 as a farmers' social organization, launched a political crusade for reforms. Electing many farm representatives to state legislatures, Grangers were able to create state railroad commissions that set maximum rates preventing discrimination against farm freight.

In the *Wabash* case of 1886, however, the Supreme Court held the railroads to be interstate enterprises beyond state control. Indignant farmers then turned to Congress for relief from this and other grievances. "We want money, land and transportation," demanded Mary Elizabeth Lease of Kansas. "We want the abolition of National Banks, and we want the power to make loans direct from the government. We want the accursed foreclosure system wiped out."

The Grange forced Congress to pass the Interstate Commerce Act of 1887, reviving many reforms that had been cancelled at the state level by the *Wabash* decision. As a further concession to farmers, Congress passed the Sherman Anti-Trust Act making illegal railroad, bank and other monopolies.

But the farmers had even more radical goals in mind. In 1891 a

Farmers' Alliance (Populist) political movement demanded government ownership of the railroads, telegraph and telephone
lines; government low-interest loans to farmers; free coinage of
silver for cheaper money; a graduated Federal income tax; lower
tariffs on manufactured products farmers had to buy; and Federal
postal savings banks.

In their first election test, the Populists polled over a million
votes, electing three senators, ten congressmen, four governors
and hundreds of lesser officials. Governor L. D. Lewelling of
Kansas, inaugurated in 1893, spelled out the farmers' insistence
that Washington must protect them: "The Government must
make it possible for the citizen to live by his own labor. . . . If
the Government fails in these things, it fails in its mission. . . .
The people are greater than the law or the statutes, and when a
nation sets its heart on doing a great or good thing, it can find a
legal way to do it."

In the next election of 1896 western and southern farmers
rallied together to "raise less corn and more Hell." Believing that
many of their financial troubles could be solved by taking the
country off the gold standard, the Populists demanded unlimited
coinage of silver so that they could pay off their debts to the
banks in cheaper, inflated money.

William Jennings Bryan became their standard-bearer on the
Democratic ticket. Republican William McKinley, who defended
the gold standard and big business, promised that the Establishment would bring back prosperity and a rise in farm prices. The
Populists were defeated in a bitter campaign during which they
were branded fanatics, Communists and revolutionaries, with big
business firms threatening employees that they would shut down
if Bryan were elected.

The election of Woodrow Wilson in 1912 brought to the White
House a President acutely aware that, while Washington had
catered to the needs of industrialists, it had treated farmers
shabbily. In December 1913 he told Congress, "We have allowed
the industry of our farms to lag behind the other activities of the
country in its development. I need not stop to tell you how
fundamental to the life of the Nation is the production of its
food. . . . We must add the means by which the farmer may
make his credit constantly and easily available. . . . We left our
farmers to shift for themselves in the ordinary money market.

You have but to look about you in any rural district to see the result, the handicap and embarrassment which have been put upon those who produce our food."

That month Congress enacted the Federal Reserve Act providing a dozen money centers in the country where there had been only one before. It broke the monopoly over the nation's finances previously exercised by Wall Street. In 1916 the Federal Loan Act provided farmers with low-cost, long-term loans through special Farm Loan Banks.

During the Harding administration farmers were hard hit by the depression that followed World War I. A farm bloc of twenty-seven senators who held the balance of power in the Senate once more raised the Populist cry against exploitation by eastern bankers, and demanded that Washington again come to the financial rescue of farmers. Harding resisted, telling Congress, "The farmer requires no special favors at the hands of the government. All he needs is a fair chance."

Although other sectors of the economy prospered during the 1920s, farm prices remained low, with farm products a glut on the market. So many farms were lost in forced sales through bankruptcies, foreclosures and tax delinquencies that Congress had to pass the Agricultural Credits Act of 1924. Loans were granted to dealers and farm cooperatives to let them buy and hold farm goods for better prices, hopefully preventing farm bankruptcies and the dumping of surpluses on the market.

But the farmers' plight only grew worse. The Senate farm bloc then won passage of the McNary-Haugen bill, which introduced a startling new idea. A proposed Federal Farm Board would purchase the annual surplus of specified commodities during years of bumper crops, and either keep this surplus off the market until prices rose, or sell it abroad at the prevailing world price. If sales abroad resulted in a government loss, farmers would owe the Farm Board that amount.

But President Calvin Coolidge vetoed the bill in 1927 on grounds that it incorporated a price-fixing principle opposed to "free enterprise" and benefited a special group.

In 1929 Congress tried establishing a Federal Farm Board with half a billion dollars to use in stabilizing farm prices, by buying when prices were low and selling when prices were high. But by 1931 the Depression and a bumper crop of huge surpluses forced the Board out of operation, with a loss to the Government of almost $400 million.

The irony of want amidst plenty drove farmers to violent action. As farm income collapsed while taxes and mortgage obligations remained high, thousands of farmers lost their farms for failure to pay taxes or meet bank payments. On a single day in April 1932, one-fourth of the entire state of Mississippi went under the hammer of auctioneers. Farmers in many states stormed auctions, guns in hand, to force bankrupt farms to be sold for such token sums as $1.18, in order to "buy" them back for their original owners.

"Right here in Mississippi some people are about ready to lead a mob," angrily declared Governor Theodore Bilbo. "In fact, I'm getting a little pink myself!"

In Iowa during the summer of 1932 farmers refused to ship food into Sioux City for a month, or until they were paid at least what it cost them to produce. Highways were blocked with logs and spiked telephone poles. Farmers punctured tires with pitchforks. When fifty-five pickets were arrested, a thousand farmers prepared to storm the jail until they were released on bail.

In Wisconsin, dairy farmers dumped milk on the road, and fought stormy battles with deputy sheriffs.

Campaigning for the farm vote in Topeka, Kansas, Franklin D. Roosevelt told farmers, "This nation cannot endure if it is half 'boom' and half 'broke'. . . . We must have, I assert with all possible emphasis, national planning in agriculture." He promised to ease farm credit to prevent mortgage foreclosures; readjust tariffs to encourage overseas sales of surplus crops; and compel local governments to cut farm taxes.

Elected, he invited all of the nation's farm organizations to come up with a program all could agree upon. Secretary of Agriculture Henry Wallace consulted with them and developed an omnibus farm bill, the Agricultural Adjustment Act. When Congress wrangled over its passage, violence broke out again in the Corn Belt. A mob of farmers masked in blue bandannas dragged Judge Charles C. Bradley from his bench in LeMars, Iowa, and nearly lynched him to compel him not to sign any more mortgage foreclosures. The Farmers' Holiday Association called a national farmers' strike for May 1933.

Alarmed, Congress whipped through the farm bill setting up an Agricultural Adjustment Administration. The AAA began paying farmers for raising fewer crops and livestock, to reduce farm surpluses; provided refinancing of farm mortgages through the Federal Land Banks; and established fair prices for basic crops. Payments to farmers came out of Federal taxes on companies processing farm products; the companies in turn passed these costs along to consumers.

Farmers collected over $100 million in benefit payments for plowing under ten million acres of surplus cotton. Over six million pigs and 200,000 sows were slaughtered to prevent a glut in the hog market. The news shocked many Americans, who indignantly criticized Henry Wallace. The Secretary of Agriculture replied acridly, "Perhaps they think that farmers should run a sort of old-folks home for hogs and keep them around indefinitely as barnyard pets." But the reputation of the AAA was tarnished by what seemed to many Americans an insane policy of destroying food while so many people went hungry. Animal lovers were upset by the AAA's "unspeakable inhumanity."

Despite the efforts of the AAA, many farm groups suffered extreme hardships. In the Great Plains region, drought devastated farmers when dust storms blew away their topsoil and compelled them to migrate to California along Highway 66.

In Arkansas sharecroppers and farm laborers were victimized by the brutal tactics of landlords and local officials in control of AAA committees. When they sought to organize the Southern Tenant Farmers' Union in July 1934, they were hunted down, flogged, jailed, shot and murdered.

"We Garded our House and been on the scout untill we are Ware out," wrote one sharecropper's wife, "and Havent any Law to looks to. thay and the Land Lords hast all turned to nite Riding . . . they shat up some Houses and have Threten our Union and Waont let us Meet at the Hall at all."

In 1937 the New Deal created the Bankhead-Jones Farm Tenant Act, establishing the Farm Security Administration. The FSA made long-term, low-interest loans to tenant farmers, sharecroppers and farm laborers whose applications were approved by local farmers' committees. Migrant workers were also protected by FSA regulations governing wages and hours, camp sanitation and medical services.

In the 1930s dust storms and bank foreclosures forced many farmers to abandon their farms and become migrant workers.
(CULVER PICTURES, INC.)

Perhaps nothing changed farm lives more during the Roosevelt era than the President's creation of the Rural Electrification Administration (REA) in May 1935. Nine out of ten American farms had no electricity—no electrically powered farm machinery and tools; no washing machines, refrigerators or vacuum cleaners; no electric lights to read by at night. Many farm families had never even seen electric light. Farm work was done laboriously by men, women and children field hands just as it had been in the days of peasantry.

Roosevelt established the REA by executive order, under powers granted him by the Emergency Relief Appropriation Act of 1935. The REA was designed to bring electricity to isolated rural areas not served by private state utilities, by offering low-cost government loans to nonprofit farmers' cooperatives. Farmers borrowed millions of dollars to electrify the countryside, which in a few years began to blaze with the spectacle of electric light. By the outset of World War II, four farms out of ten had electricity. By the end of that decade power lines had reached nine farms out of ten.

Not surprisingly, in the election year of 1936, once-Republican farm states turned Democratic. Farm prices were up; electrification was becoming a reality for millions of farm families; foreclosures were growing rare. Although farmers acknowledged their debt to Washington, they were irritated by the supervision of Federal agents in the AAA program.

"They don't like to be checked up on by Washington," noted *New York Times* columnist Arthur Krock in December 1935, "even though they signed agreements that this should be done. If the Republicans can devise some way to produce the same farm prices, and do away with the domination and inspection of Washington, they will have made a move toward getting their natural areas back in the party fold."

A food processor named Butler, resenting the tax he had to pay to the AAA for the benefit of farmers, went to court to challenge it. In 1936 the Supreme Court invalidated the whole AAA program as unconstitutional (*U.S. v. Butler et al.*). Justice Owen J. Roberts declared that a tax used to regulate agricultural production infringed upon state powers: "The word [tax] has never been thought to connote the expropriation of money from one group for the benefit of another."

This upset decision was one of a series by an ultraconservative Supreme Court that convinced Roosevelt the country could never recover fully from the Depression until the Court could be liberalized. His attempt to "stack the Court" by appointing additional justices was defeated by Congress, which undid the Court's damage by passing a Soil Conservation and Domestic Allotment Act (1936) and a second AAA Act (1938).

The second AAA restored price supports and provided for production controls when necessary, but eliminated the tax on processors. The Supreme Court, by this time liberalized by new appointments replacing retiring justices, upheld the AAA as a constitutional regulation of interstate commerce.

In the years that followed, Washington's help to the farmer was vitiated by two developments—manipulation of agricultural programs for the benefit of big corporation farms, rather than little farmers; and in the South, for the benefit of white, but not poor black, farmers.

"Because the decision of who can grow what on how many acres is left strictly up to white southerners," observed Robert Sherrill in his book, *Gothic Politics in the Deep South*, "it is not surprising that white farmers are getting wealthier and the emigration of broke and hungry Negro farmers to the slums of the North and West continues. Mississippi lost 40 per cent of its tenant farmers between 1959 and 1964. . . . The seeds of ghetto rioting are planted by the U.S. Department of Agriculture on the abandoned Negro farms of the South."

The Federal farm program was also faulted for contradictory operations. In 1969, while spending $200 million to help farmers increase their production, the Agriculture Department also paid out $3.5 billion in subsidies to farmers to reduce surpluses by not overplanting acreages allotted to them.

The benefits of the farm program were unevenly divided. Of ten million people living on the nation's three million farms in 1969, two million were aging couples no longer able to work, poorly housed and fed, lacking sewers, pure water and adequate medical care. Most of the $3.5 billion in farm subsidies were paid to the top one-third of farmers—approximately one million—which included the wealthier planters.

George Mehrant, a small South Carolina farmer, received less than $200 in Federal aid for working his ninety-seven acres. At the same time in Los Angeles, James G. Boswell received over $4 million in Federal subsidies to supplement his income from his vast farm operations in California and Arizona.

Neither case was unique. According to *New York Times* reporter William Robbins, "Mr. Mehrant was one of 1 million farmers, most of them below the poverty level, whose federal payments averaged less than $400 each. Although prosperous, Mr. Boswell was one of seven farmers receiving more than $1 million in federal aid and one of nearly 8,500 well-to-do planters who received more than $25,000 in subsidy checks."

The explanation: "The farm programs have been perpetuated by a group of men in Congress who exercise powers out of proportion to their numbers, and who have been fearful that social-action programs benefiting the broad spectrum of rural people might drain off funds now going to implement agricultural legislation. . . . Their sympathies have tended to go out to the larger landowners." One such powerful "farmer" was Senator James Eastland of Mississippi, owner of a cotton plantation that received $200,000 a year in Federal subsidies.

The subsidy system, instead of preserving family farms, tended to raise land prices to levels that induced small farmers to sell out to big corporate farms, and leave to seek jobs in the cities. In February 1973 President Nixon proposed the gradual elimination of subsidy programs, beginning with payments of certain direct subsidies received mostly by small farmers. "The farmer wants, has earned and deserves more freedom to make his own decisions," he told Congress.

The President believed that with higher prices for farm products, the farmers of America should be prepared to compete without either aid or controls from Washington. At his request the Agriculture Department abolished several key farm programs. An angry Congress voted to restore them.

In 1972 the President arranged a huge sale of grain to the Soviet Union. Senator George McGovern accused the Agriculture Department of tipping off grain-exporting companies in advance, to enable them to buy up wheat at low prices from unsuspecting farmers who didn't know about the sale. Spokesmen for the small farmers were bitter, convinced that once again the Agriculture Department had acted in the interests of the corporate farms and grain dealers, not in theirs.

Senator Gaylord Nelson of Wisconsin sponsored a bill in June 1973 aimed at ending handouts to the corporate farms, which Senator Fred Harris of Oklahoma had described as "more efficient at farming Washington." Nelson charged the Agriculture Department with concealing from the public the extent to which big corporations had taken over agriculture and received the bulk of billions spent in farm aid programs.

Even though farmers in general enjoyed a boom in rising prices during 1973, there seemed little likelihood that Washington would reverse its role as protector of the farmer in all fifty states of the Union. "Without some aid in the way of price supports," insisted Georgia's Herman Talmadge, chairman of the powerful Senate Agriculture Committee, "virtually every small farmer in America would be plowed under."

With a growing world demand for American farm products added to increased consumption at home, Congress prepared to pass a new farm bill that would encourage greater production by offering farmers guaranteed prices for basic commodities, with a $20,000 ceiling on agricultural subsidies that could be paid to any one farm family or unit.

13 · Who protects labor?

*P*ressured by big business lobbies, the Texas state legislature passes a new antilabor bill. Union organizers are prohibited from recruiting members within Texas borders without first registering with, and obtaining a license from, the Texas Secretary of State. The news creates indignation among national labor unions. R. J. Thomas, president of the United Automobile Workers, announces that he is going to Texas to address a union meeting in defiance of the law.

When he does so, without registering or securing a permit, he is promptly arrested and convicted. But in a 1945 appeal to the Supreme Court, the Texan antilabor statute is declared unconstitutional. "A requirement of registration in order to make a public speech," rules the Court, "would seem generally incompatible with an exercise of the rights of free speech and assembly" (*Thomas v. Collins*).

State legislatures and state courts have traditionally shown far more concern for the rights of industry than for the rights of labor, compelling the unions to look primarily to Washington for protection. Only a handful of states have minimum wage laws. Eighteen have "right-to-work" laws prohibiting the union shop or compulsory union membership.

"It is not surprising, therefore," observes University of Illinois political analyst Jack W. Peltason, "to find that businessmen's organizations are quick to defend the states against what they characterize as the 'federal octopus,' while labor leaders emphasize the need for national action and charge the states with being dominated by 'special interests.' "

In 1829 the New York State Assembly passed a law making it a conspiracy "to commit any act injurious to . . . trade or commerce." Six years later when shoemakers in Geneva, New York, struck a shop paying under the minimum union wage, the state Supreme Court found them guilty of conspiracy, and declared it illegal for workers to combine to raise wages.

In Maryland, Irish laborers constructing the Chesapeake and Ohio Canal struck for a closed shop in 1834. When the company brought in strikebreakers, stormy clashes led the governor of Maryland to call upon President Andrew Jackson for help. The President ordered the War Department to put down the "riotous assembly"—the first use of Federal troops to intervene in a state labor dispute.

One year later a New York court declared all strikes illegal (*People v. Fisher*). But the Supreme Court of Massachusetts ruled for its state that trade unions, and strikes for a closed shop, were legal (*Commonwealth v. Hunt*, 1841). There was virtually no Federal legislation governing labor relations; the vacuum was filled by many repressive state laws.

Even after the Sherman Anti-Trust Law (1890) and its companion Clayton Act (1914) were passed to break up monopolies, this Federal legislation was ironically used instead to outlaw strikes as "in restraint of interstate commerce." From 1883 on, both Federal and state court injunctions were often used to smash strikes under one pretext or another.

Washington's bias against labor unions reached a peak under business-dominated administrations like that of President Grover Cleveland, when Attorney General Richard Olney acted as a Federal strikebreaker for the railroad interests.

In 1894 Eugene V. Debs led the independent American Railway Union in a strike against the Pullman Company which tied up every midwestern railroad. Olney swore in 3,400 special deputies to break the strike under the pretexts of preserving order, insuring delivery of the U.S. mails, and protecting interstate commerce. He also sent Federal troops to Chicago, where violence had broken out. Later investigation established

Soldiers escorting a train during the Pullman Strike of 1894.

that the violence there had been largely the work of agents provocateurs who were hired by the railroads to discredit the strike.

The liberal-minded governor of Illinois, John Altgeld, protested to President Cleveland against the invasion of his state by Federal troops. Local police and state militia, he insisted, were well able to cope with the Chicago disturbances. If the President could send troops to any part of the country on his own decision, he could destroy local self-government as easily as any czar or emperor.

"Great precautions have been taken to limit the use of such power," Altgeld declared, because the American people were "jealous of a central military power." At a rally of 10,000 workers in New York City, reformer Henry George evoked a storm of applause by vowing, "I would rather see every locomotive in this land ditched, every car and every depot burned and every rail torn up, than to have them preserved by means of a Federal standing army!"

Federal Judge Peter Grosscup, who owed his appointment to the influence of railroad magnates, issued an injunction against the "conspiratorial" strikers. When they refused to call off their strike, Debs and other strike leaders were jailed for contempt of court and held behind bars without a jury trial until the strike had been smashed.

A national uproar over Washington's role in breaking the strike compelled Cleveland to appoint a commission to investigate labor's charges against Olney.

Debs testified:

"When the authorities are called upon to intercede in troubles of this kind," he demanded, "do they ever ask labor a question? Never! . . . When and where did the militia ever come out and take its stand on the side of labor, to prevent the workingmen's being robbed and degraded? Never! . . . They have gone into partnership with the oppressors of labor to crush labor."

Big business sympathizers attacked Governor Altgeld for opposing the use of Federal troops. Theodore Roosevelt, who later sought votes as a self-styled "trust-buster," declared, "Mr. Altgeld condones and encourages the most infamous of murders, and denounces the Federal Government and the Supreme Court for interfering to put a stop to the bloody lawlessness which would result in worse than murder."

Roosevelt failed to criticize the Pullman Company, which had slashed its workers' wages by up to forty per cent while giving its stockholders an eight per cent dividend; and which compelled workers to live in a company town, overcharging them for rent, gas and water in tenements without bathtubs, and with only one water faucet for every five flats.

Labor leaders suffered another Federal setback after they had pressured the New York state legislature into passing a law limiting bakery employees to a sixty-hour week, to protect their health from the effects of long hours amidst hot ovens. To avoid higher labor costs by adding more employees, bakery owners fought the law to the U.S. Supreme Court.

"There is no reasonable ground for interfering with the liberty of person or the right of free contract, by determining the hours of labor, in the occupation of a baker," ruled Justice Rufus W. Peckham. ". . . The act is not, within any fair meaning of the term, a health law, but is an illegal interference with the rights of individuals, both employers and employees, to make contracts regarding labor upon such terms as they may think best. . . . [Laws] limiting the hours in which grown and intelligent men may labor to earn their living, are mere meddlesome interferences" (*Lochner v. New York*, 1905).

Bakery employees were understandably unenthusiastic about this Federal defense of their right to work "as long as they wanted" in the blistering infernos of the bakeshops.

The ultraconservative tilt of the Supreme Court of that day was underscored in 1908 in what became known as the Danbury Hatters' Case. When the hatters' union sought to win a strike by establishing a secondary boycott of firms dealing with the struck company, the Court cited the Sherman Anti-Trust Act to hold the union guilty of a conspiracy in restraint of trade (*Loewe v. Lawlor*).

Sweatshop labor was the order of the day. Dr. Howard Woolston, Director of Investigation for the New York State Factory Commission, revealed, "More than half the people employed in the factories and stores investigated in New York City get less than $8.00 a week."

Not until 1916 did labor have a friend in the White House. Woodrow Wilson sponsored the Adamson Act limiting the workday to eight hours on railroads operating in interstate commerce. The law was challenged by the railroads in the Supreme Court, but Chief Justice Edward D. White upheld its constitutionality, giving great impetus to the eight-hour-day movement throughout the country (*Wilson v. New*, 1917).

The status of child labor in many states was indicated in 1916 by former Governor William Hitchin, who defended the ten-hour workday for children in North Carolina: "The cotton mill furnishes an opportunity for light and remunerative work for the children. Children twelve and fourteen years old can do just as good work as a thirty-year-old man . . . and help take care of the family. I think that is a blessing." Companies paying them half the adult rate certainly thought so.

One company doctor insisted, "You couldn't fix an age limit for child labor any more than you could tell when a pig becomes a hog." David Clark, editor of the *Southern Textile Bulletin*, scoffed at the idea of taking children out of the mills and putting them in school: "When these people come from the mountains they do not believe in education. That is the reason we do not have compulsory education in North Carolina."

Because of the lack of Federal child labor legislation, states like North Carolina were able to lure away employers from other states with a cheap child labor supply. So in 1916 Congress sought to stop industrial raiding by passing the Keating-Owen Child Labor Act, barring the products of child labor from interstate commerce.

The new law upset one North Carolina father of two teen-age sons who worked in a Charlotte cotton mill and stood to lose their jobs. With the backing of the state's millowners, he challenged the law up to the Supreme Court. It was defended by the U.S. Solicitor General, who pointed out that working in factories stunted children's growth and health, also subjecting them to diseases and industrial accidents. And he stressed the unfairness of letting some states use cheap child labor to undersell others with humane laws.

But the Court, taking a strict interpretation of the Constitution, struck down the law. While admitting that child labor was a social evil, Justice William R. Day declared, "The necessary effect of this act is . . . to regulate the hours of labor of children in factories and mines within the States, a purely state authority" (*Hammer v. Dagenhart*, 1918).

The practical result of this decision was to render Federal regulation of child labor all but impossible until a changed Court later reversed the verdict in 1941.

The state of Kansas passed sweeping labor laws in 1920 "solving" industrial disputes by abolishing the right to strike, picket or boycott in key industries, and setting up a court of industrial relations with the power to fix wages and working conditions, its decisions compulsory. But the Supreme Court ruled the laws in violation of the Fourteenth Amendment.

In 1922 when the Interstate Commerce Commission ordered the railroads to reduce their rates by ten per cent, the carriers won permission from the Railroad Labor Board to slash workers' pay by twelve and one half per cent. Over 400,000 railroad shopmen struck in protest. The Railroad Labor Board branded their strike illegal, because it was against a government tribunal. When the railroads brought in strikebreakers and armed guards, violence flared. Other railroad workers struck.

On a single day a dozen continental trains suddenly stopped in the Arizona desert, and 2,500 passengers found themselves marooned as crews of the Santa Fe Railroad abandoned their trains. At Needles, California, one train was stranded for four days in 113-degree heat. Some children and old people collapsed, and some babies were born in the cars.

Public opinion was outraged. President Warren Harding condemned the lawlessness growing out of the strike, and announced his resolve to "use the power of the Government to maintain transportation and sustain the right of the [nonunion] men to work." He blamed state authorities for not using force to suppress the labor disorders.

Attorney General Harry Daugherty accused the Shopmen's Union of being manipulated by "Red borers" to compel the government to take over the railroads. He sought to break the strike with a Federal court injunction that forbade strikers from "loitering" or "congregating" near yards, shops, depots or terminals; from picketing; or from talking to scabs.

Republican Congressman Jackson Ralston of Minnesota introduced a resolution in the House to impeach the Attorney General for high crimes and misdemeanors in "abridging freedom of speech, freedom of the press, the right of the people peaceably to assemble." He also noted acidly that Daugherty had failed to prosecute any big business lawbreakers.

Daugherty charged all those against him with being part of a vast Red plot. His injunction broke the strike.

In 1930 Senator George Norris of Nebraska visited the Pennsylvania coalfields. He saw miners living in hovels and shacktowns and working under dangerous conditions. The state's venal sheriffs, unfriendly courts and arrogant mine owners cooperated to enforce what Norris called "a type of bondage that enslaved the miner." Workers were compelled to sign "yellow-dog" contracts, prohibiting them from joining unions. The Supreme Court had upheld such contracts in 1908 on grounds that union membership was not covered by interstate commerce laws (*Adair v. U.S.*).

Outraged, Norris introduced the Norris-LaGuardia Anti-Injunction Act forbidding court injunctions to sustain yellow-dog contracts, or to prevent strikes, boycotts and picketing. Passed overwhelmingly by a Congress sensitive to union pressure in a deepening Depression, the bill was signed reluctantly by President Herbert Hoover. It was the first of a new series of prolabor Federal laws of the 1930s that marked a turning point in Washington's attitude toward labor rights.

Alabama Senator Hugo Black, seeking to create another six million jobs, introduced a bill to bar from interstate commerce goods produced in any plant that worked its employees more than thirty hours a week. William Green, head of the AFL, threatened a general strike if Congress did not pass the Black bill. The Senate voted for it, but President Roosevelt preferred his own solution to the unemployment problem.

In June 1933 he rammed through Congress a sweeping National Industrial Recovery Act. The NIRA laid down Federal guidelines for industrial operations and competition; Section 7a guaranteed labor's right "to organize and bargain collectively through representatives of their own choosing."

A test case soon rose in Brooklyn, N.Y., where the Schechter brothers owned a small slaughterhouse and bought chickens from out of state to sell in and around New York City. They were indicted for violating requirements of the Live Poultry Code of the NIRA by paying less than the fifty-cent-an-hour minimum wage; working employees over forty hours a week; and selling diseased chicken without the required inspection.

Convicted by the highest Federal court in New York State, the brothers appealed to the Supreme Court. The decision handed down in 1935 came as a stunning blow to President Roosevelt and most Americans, if not to the business community. A unanimous Supreme Court not only overturned the conviction, but also held the entire NIRA unconstitutional (*Schecter Poultry Corp. v. United States*).

No President or Congress, Chief Justice Charles Evans Hughes declared, was "at liberty to transcend the imposed limits [of the Constitution] because they believe that more or different power is necessary. . . . The authority of the federal government may not be pushed to such an extreme."

Congress replaced major parts of the NIRA by new legislation such as the Wagner Labor Act of 1935—a bill of rights for unions. It guaranteed the right of collective bargaining; legalized strikes and boycotts; and set rules compelling employers to bargain with unions in good faith. A National Labor Relations

Board (NLRB) was authorized to hold union elections and investigate union complaints.

Big labor, in one giant step, almost gained equality with big business for the first time in American history. The CIO broke away from the AFL to begin organizing the auto and steel industries, staging spectacular sit-down strikes in the plants to compel collective bargaining.

In 1936 the New Deal Congress passed the Walsh-Healey Act requiring all companies with Federal contracts, or with state contracts involving Federal grants, to observe Federal standards for wages, hours and working conditions.

When the NLRB sought to regulate labor conditions in the huge Jones & Laughlin steel plant, that outraged company refused to comply with its orders. The case reached the Supreme Court in 1937, with the company arguing that the workers involved were not directly connected with the shipment of goods, and therefore not a proper Federal concern under the interstate commerce power. But the Court upheld the government position that labor was a part of the "stream of commerce," which in the case of steel began with shipments of iron ore and ended with deliveries of the finished product (*National Labor Relations Board v. Jones and Laughlin Steel Corporation*).

In 1938 a Fair Labor Standards (Black-Connery) Act passed under Roosevelt's leadership, after a bitter struggle within the Democratic Party between northern and southern Congressmen. The act established a national forty-hour week maximum, and a forty-cent-an-hour minimum wage, with time and a half for overtime. Shipment of any products of child labor was once more banned from interstate commerce.

Seeking to stem the tide of unionization, many corporations warned employees that joining unions might cost them their jobs. In a test case that reached the Supreme Court, employers argued that their right to free speech was just as fully protected under the Constitution as that of their employees. But Justice Frank Murphy agreed with the NLRB that coercive conduct by an employer towards his workers was not protected by the First Amendment (*Labor Board v. Virginia Power Co.*).

Following World War II, the United Mine Workers called a strike of 400,000 coal miners. President Harry S. Truman seized the mines from the recalcitrant coal companies, which would not bargain in good faith with the union, and Federal negotiators worked out a contract. The coal companies refused to accept it, so Washington kept control of the mines.

In November union leader John L. Lewis called another strike. Truman promptly secured a court injunction to end it as an illegal strike against the Government. Defying the injunction, Lewis was held in contempt of court and fined $10,000. The union was fined $3,500,000, later reduced to $700,000. Both fines were upheld by the Supreme Court.

Although labor unions had made enormous gains during the New Deal, in 1947 the pendulum swung backward with the passage of the Taft-Hartley Act. A conservative Congress overrode Truman's veto. The new Federal law banned the closed shop; permitted employers to sue unions for broken contracts or for strike damage; required unions to abide by a court order for a sixty-day "cooling-off period" before striking; compelled unions to make their finances public; ended the "check-off system" requiring employers to collect union dues; and made union leaders take an oath that they were not Communists.

At the state level, "little Taft-Hartley laws" were also passed to restrict union activity. Some states prohibited the union shop, the closed shop and the requirement of a union card to hold a job. The Supreme Court upheld these state "right-to-work" laws.

Texas outlawed picket lines in which demonstrators followed each other at less than fifty feet apart. Any demonstrator arrested on a picket line was known thereafter under Texas law as a felon and forbidden to hold union office. Union officers and organizers were compelled to register with the state and to carry special identification cards. Texas Governor Allan Shivers even sought a state law making membership in the Communist Party punishable by a death sentence.

Not surprisingly, out of two and a half million nonagricultural Texas workers in 1956, only about fifteen per cent had been recruited as members of labor unions.

When it became apparent that many unions, as well as employers, were discriminating against blacks and other minorities, Congress in 1964 passed civil rights legislation setting up an Equal Employment Opportunity Commission with power to investigate and act upon complaints. Some states set up Fair Employment Practices Commissions of their own.

One large group of American workers who felt aggrieved and mistreated, both on the Federal and state level, were public service workers. Forbidden by law to strike, they had no real leverage to win cost-of-living raises. In March 1970, over 6,000 New York letter carriers walked off the job in the first large-scale strike in the U.S. Postal Service's 195-year history. Defying a Federal court injunction ordering them back to work, they were joined by letter clerks and carriers in other cities until almost 200,000 were involved. Millions of pieces of undelivered mail piled up.

Declaring a state of emergency, President Nixon assigned troops to get the mail moving again in the key bottleneck of New York. Postal workers vowed that if their demands were not met, they would continue striking "until hell freezes over." They finally consented to return to work on a solemn congressional promise to vote them a twelve per cent wage hike.

The states experienced similar problems with civil service employees. In dozens of municipal and state agencies across the country, policemen, firemen, sanitation workers and others struck illegally until they were promised or given raises and improved

Federal troops were called in to replace striking postal workers in 1970.
(WERNER WOLFF, BLACK STAR)

conditions. Nothing was done to punish police of the New York Port Authority, nor toll collectors on New York's parkways, when they walked off their jobs in July 1973, causing massive traffic snarls and tie-ups.

Workers today most in need of help from Washington are ethnic minorities on the bottom of the economic ladder like Cesar Chavez's Mexican-American grape pickers and underpaid Puerto Rican hospital workers. Their problem, to a large extent, is discrimination against them by predominantly white labor unions. Congress and some state legislatures have tried to help by passing protective legislation.

The Nixon administration and the four Nixon appointees to the Supreme Court were not sympathetic to the idea of more protective Federal labor legislation. The President preferred to leave such legislation up to the states and cities. In September 1973 he vetoed a higher minimum wage passed by Congress.

But he did little to prevent rising prices and profits, causing AFL-CIO labor chief George Meany, who had supported him, to denounce the President as a protector of big business interests at the expense of American workers. "Under the Nixon so-called Economic Stabilization Program, only workers' wages remain stringently controlled," Meany complained in January 1974. "The economy is an absolute mess."

14 · Who protects the consumer?

*M*rs. *Katherine Ringenbach of Tucson, Arizona,* is upset because a package she mailed three months ago still hasn't been delivered. Fearing it may have been lost in the mails, she inquires at her local post office in March 1973.

"Don't worry about it, lady," a harried postal clerk tells her. "We're still delivering Christmas mail!"

Mrs. Ringenbach is not alone in her exasperation with the quality of mail service she buys with high-priced postage stamps from the now semiprivate U.S. Postal Service. People who get letters from Australia in three days can't understand why it takes local mail two to three days just to travel across town. Airmail from Columbus, Ohio, to Chicago—a one-hour flight—takes five days to arrive. Lawyers are missing court appearances because legal notices don't arrive in time.

Over 600 complaints a week pour into Washington. The new head of the U.S. Postal Service, which now employs 64,000 fewer employees to handle the mail as an economy measure, refuses to accept the blame. "The deterioration of postal operations didn't begin with the creation of the U.S. Postal Service," he insists, adding, "The mess that Congress has now decided to investigate is largely a mess of its own making."

Meanwhile irate citizens can do nothing but laugh wryly at the satirist who dramatizes their frustration by reintroducing the Pony Express. Mailing Special Delivery Airmail letters to a town

· 163

Consumer advocate Ralph Nader testifying before a House committee.
(WIDE WORLD PHOTOS)

100 miles away, he takes copies with him to the same address by ponyback. No one is surprised when he arrives at the destination two days ahead of the mailed letters.

Today's consumers often find themselves faced with a bewildering deterioration in the American life style, and it seems impossible to fix the blame or get anything done about it. In 1974 consumers complained of runaway food prices, shrinking contents of food packages, gas and home fuel oil shortages, skyrocketing medical costs and the sale of contaminated foods and dangerous drugs. Who protects the consumer?

Congress is slow to accept this responsibility because many of the corporations that victimize consumers are also important contributors to congressmen's election campaign funds and their lobbies also perform other favors. "The time is fast approaching, I am convinced," said Texas Congressman Wright Patman, "when Congress must decide just how far it is willing to go to allow these lobbyists to go on influencing legislation."

Only in recent years has the consumer been represented in Washington by a small lobby of his own. John Gardner's Common Cause and Ralph Nader's "Nader's Raiders" have sought to offset big business pressure on Congress by pressing for bills benefiting the consumer. But these are often pigeonholed, delayed or weakened by powerful committee chairmen.

Protecting the consumer from inferior or harmful products is supposed to be assured by Federal watchdog commissions supervising big business. If advertising of a cold remedy or TV set is misleading, the Federal Trade Commission (FTC) presumably stops it. Improperly labeled and unsafe foods and drugs are supposed to be taken off the market by the Food and Drug Administration (FDA). Federal regulatory commissions, however, have often been criticized by consumer groups as more protective of negligent industries than of consumers.

Through most of the nineteenth century, as private corporations played an increasingly important part in the nation's development, there was a constant struggle between monopolies and consumers. In 1828 Bostonians grew tired of paying a toll to the Charles Bridge Company every time they used its bridge to cross the Charles River. They compelled the Massachusetts legislature to charter another company to build an adjacent bridge which would be toll-free after costs were recovered.

The Charles Bridge Company sued for an injunction, charging that its own forty-three-year-old charter had been violated. When the case went to the Supreme Court in 1837, Chief Justice Roger B. Taney ruled that monopoly had to bow to competition for the benefit of consumers. "While the rights of private property are sacredly guarded," he said, "we must not forget that the community also have rights, and that the happiness and well-being of every citizen depends on their faithful preservation."

In 1840 the House Committee on Public Lands reported that land barons were stealing land grants away from small property-owners by legal trickery involving deception, perjury and fraud. "Redress through the courts . . . is slow and expensive," the Committee found. "The persons aggrieved are generally men poor in purse, living by their labor, and they have not the means to contend in court with wrongdoers."

Congress failed to stop the practice. Even when it passed legislation threatening jail and fines for big lumber corporations that illegally cut timber on public lands, the law was generally ignored or evaded. In the Minnesota Black River region, sixteen lumber mills prospered by harvesting public pines as bribed Federal timber agents looked the other way.

When one honest Michigan agent indicted thirty-seven companies for timber violations in 1854, they hired gangs to prevent government seizure of the stolen lumber while they sailed it off in lake ships. Arguing before the Supreme Court, their lawyers insisted that timber was not a part of the land, so that the Federal law against cutting timber on public lands was illegal. But the Court held, "The timber while standing is part of the realty" (*U.S. v. Cook*).

When Congress began giving public grants of western lands to homesteaders on a large scale, realty sharks successfully lobbied for provisions in the legislation that let them acquire huge land grants fraudulently and cheaply.

"The poor settler had very little opportunity to secure land," noted historian Gustavus Myers. "Almost wherever he appeared he was confronted by the capitalists who claimed vast stretches of land—agricultural, grazing, mineral and timber." Secretary of the Interior Jacob Thompson reported to President James Buchanan in 1859, "Unscrupulous speculators profit by it more than any other class."

With the growth of the big corporations following the Civil War, profits were sought ruthlessly by cheating, deceiving and defrauding consumers on the principle of *caveat emptor*—let the buyer beware. Consumers found their state legislatures weak reeds to lean on for protection. Key legislators were often bribed to vote state subsidies to railroad, oil, coal and timber corporations. "I think I can say, and say with pride," Mark Twain observed dryly, "that we have the best legislatures that money can buy."

The consumer was also ill-served by the eager rivalry between states for the taxes and jobs that corporations provided as resident industries. Each state offered a maximum of inducements and a minimum of restrictions for plants to locate within its boundaries. The weaker the restraints, the more corporations were free to adulterate their products, charge exorbitant prices and otherwise defraud consumers.

Most consumers were unaware of how badly they were being served by the food and drugs they bought until "muckraking" journalists, in the latter part of the nineteenth century, began exposing the unscrupulous adulteration of food, especially meat, and the fraudulent claims of useless and dangerous drugs. Public indignation forced state legislatures to pass laws penalizing the sale of such food and drugs, but the big corporations easily saw to it that these laws went unenforced.

The better to gouge the public, the big corporations banded together in monopolies they called trusts. Consumer pressure compelled some states to enact antitrust laws, but these had little effect on the practices and growth of corporations whose operations and power were national in scope.

Associations of farmers and small businessmen turned to Washington. In 1887 they compelled Congress to extend Federal power to the control of railroad, bank and business monopolies. An Interstate Commerce Act put all companies doing business across state lines under Federal supervision.

In 1890 Congress passed the Sherman Anti-Trust Act. The trusts made sure that it was so loosely worded, however, that it did little to stop the growth of monopolies. The few powerful "robber barons" who controlled meat-packing, sugar, tobacco, steel, copper, railroads and oil continued to fix prices, crush competition and indulge in other monopoly practices that plundered the consumer's pockets.

Enforcement of the Sherman Act was sabotaged by a pro-business Supreme Court. When suit was brought against the Sugar Trust, the Court ruled, incredibly, that its control of ninety-five per cent of the nation's sugar refining did not constitute a violation of the antitrust law.

"The fact that an article is manufactured for export to another State," insisted Chief Justice Melville Fuller, "does not of itself make it an article of interstate commerce." By tortuous reasoning he held that manufacturing was not commerce but only the process *before* commerce began. Sugar refining, therefore, was subject only to state regulation (*U.S. v. E. C. Knight Co.*, 1895).

By extension of Fuller's decision, every other product manufactured by the monopolies was similarly exempt from antitrust prosecution. Justice John Marshall Harlan dissented, insisting, "The common government of all the people is the only one that can adequately deal with a matter which directly and injuriously affects . . . all the people of the Union, and which, it must be confessed, cannot be adequately controlled by any one State."

The *Knight* case had been weakly prosecuted on behalf of the public by Attorney General Richard Olney, a friend of the trusts, who was pleased to lose it. "You will observe that the government has been defeated," he wrote to his secretary, ". . . I have always supposed it would and have taken the responsibility of not prosecuting [other cases] under a law I believed to be no good."

In the early 1900s rising public anger against the American big businessman was dramatized by muckraker Lincoln Steffens, who wrote, "I found him buying boodlers in St. Louis, defending grafters in Minneapolis, originating corruption in Pittsburg, sharing with bosses in Philadelphia, deploring reform in Chicago, and beating good government with corruption funds in New York. He is a self-righteous fraud, this big business man. He is the chief source of corruption."

The American middle class, fearing that public wrath might explode in riots, launched a consumer movement calling for Federal restraints on monopoly. Theodore Roosevelt, bidding for the White House, sought to make himself its leader, while privately assuring magnates whose support he needed that his antitrust bark would be worse than his bite.

After his election he pressed a suit which allowed him to claim redemption of his campaign pledge to "bust the trusts." When millionaires E. H. Harriman, James J. Hill and J. P. Morgan formed a trust to control western railroads and force users to pay monopoly rates, Roosevelt's attorney general filed an antitrust suit. In 1904 the Supreme Court ordered the trust dissolved (*Northern Securities Co. v. United States*).

He also prosecuted the Beef Trust, whose dissolution was upheld by the Supreme Court in 1905 (*Swift & Co. v. U.S.*). And a year later Congress passed the Pure Food and Drug Act, along with the Meat Inspection Act. But Roosevelt made no effort to interfere with or break up two of the nation's biggest and most powerful monopolies—the oil and tobacco trusts.

Nothing was done, either, to curb the public utilities, which were gouging consumers by exorbitant gas, electricity and water rates. In 1907 both New York and Wisconsin established the first regulatory commissions to ride herd on the utilities. But the powerful utilities made sure that the state commissions were starved for funds and hamstrung by legislation crippling their authority over rates and service.

Not until the Taft administration was consumer pressure strong enough to force Federal antitrust suits against the Standard Oil and American Tobacco trusts. In 1911 the Supreme Court upheld the dissolution of the Oil Trust as an illegal monopoly (*Standard Oil Co. of New Jersey et al. v. U.S.*). The Tobacco Trust was ordered to reorganize according to a "rule of reason" (*U.S. v. American Tobacco Co.*).

Trying to get back in the White House in 1912, Theodore Roosevelt once more played trustbuster, urging strict regulation by Washington. "The worst of the big trusts have always . . . [been] in favor of having the States themselves, and not the Nation, attempt to do this work," he noted accurately, "because they know that in the long run such effort would be ineffective. . . . The only effective way in which to regulate the trusts is through the exercise of the collective power of our people as a whole through the Governmental agencies."

When Woodrow Wilson won the White House instead, he, too, promised Federal protection against the trusts. In his First Inaugural he declared, "There can be no equality or opportunity, the first essential of justice . . . if men and women be not shielded in their lives from the consequences of great industrial and social processes which they cannot alter, control, or singly cope with."

He sought to curb the monopolies less for the protection of the consumer, however, than to assure small businessmen the right to compete in a free market. Wielding Federal power strongly, he set up a Federal Reserve System to break the monopoly of Eastern banks on loans to small businessmen; won passage of the Clayton Anti-Trust Act forbidding companies to buy or own competitors' stocks; and created a Federal Trade Commission to curb unscrupulous competition by big chains and corporations against small businesses.

Senator Elihu Root of New York protested, "The habit of undue interference by government in private affairs breeds the habit of undue reliance upon government. . . . Weaken individual character among a people by comfortable reliance upon paternal government and a nation soon becomes incapable of free self-government and fit only to be governed."

The Republican twenties once more freed the hands of the big corporations, while a conservative Supreme Court rendered frequent decisions curbing government power to regulate business. In a typical ruling the Court held that, simply because a business affected the public interest, a state legislature was not justified in seeking to regulate it unless it were a total monopoly (*Wolff Packing Co. v. Court of Industrial Relations*, 1921).

FDR's New Deal brought a whole flood of new legislation protecting the public interest against big business iniquities. In 1933 Wall Street itself fell under Federal regulation for the first time when the ("Truth In") Securities Act put a stop to the fleecing of small investors by financial manipulations beyond the control of the states.

Some states joined the Federal bandwagon by passing their own consumer protection laws. New York fixed milk prices to prevent the big dairy companies and combines from gouging the public. When the dairy interests fought this regulation up to the Supreme Court, Justice Owen J. Roberts ruled, "The Constitution does not guarantee the unrestricted privilege to engage in a business or to conduct it as one pleases. . . . Upon proper occasion and by appropriate measures the state may regulate a business or any of its aspects, including the prices to be charged" (*Nebbia v. New York*).

In 1935 the New Deal Congress passed the Public Utility Holding Company Act which stopped monopolies from charging exorbitant gas and electricity rates. A "death sentence" ordered the breakup of any holding company which could not, after five years, prove that it was both a purely local operation and in the public interest.

Outraged protests from utility and other holding company executives led the President to scoff, "The same man who tells you that he does not want to see the government interfere in business . . . is the first to go to Washington and ask the government for a prohibitory tariff on his product . . . and ask for a loan."

Roosevelt took an immense step forward in the protection of the average American by the Social Security Act of 1935. It provided unemployment compensation on a Federal-state basis; Federal old age and survivors' insurance; grants-in-aid to the states for old-age pensions, the blind, the crippled and other needy segments of society.

Conservatives denounced this Federal "cradle-to-the-grave"

security program as total interference by Washington in the private affairs of Main Street. But the Act was held constitutional in Supreme Court tests in 1937 (*Steward Machine Co. v. Davis* and *Helvering et al. v. Davis*).

At the onset of World War II, Congress passed the Emergency Price Control Act of 1942. Regulating prices and rents for the duration of the war, it protected consumers from being victimized by shortages of food, products and dwellings.

Governor Coke Stevenson of Texas refused to cooperate with a Federal gas rationing program. Texas oilmen had no objections, on the other hand, to cooperating with a state commission that regulated their industry. The commission set production quotas to hold down the amount of oil available, thus keeping prices high, as a "conservation measure." A Federal district court ruled this quota system illegal in certain Texas areas.

The Governor angrily declared martial law in those areas, ordering the state militia to enforce the quotas. But the Supreme Court ruled that since there was no riot or insurrection in Texas, martial law was illegal (*Sterling v. Constantin*).

Thanks to a powerful oil lobby in Congress, oilmen enjoyed all the advantages of a trust. They won a twenty-seven and a half per cent tax depletion allowance, of which President Harry S Truman said "no loophole in the tax law is so inequitable." Senator Robert A. Taft of Ohio observed, "Percentage depletion is to a large extent . . . a special privilege beyond what anyone else can get." Senator Paul Douglas of Illinois pointed out that some oil companies had net incomes of over $12 million and didn't pay a cent in taxes; some even received a $500,000 tax credit from the Federal government. Yet postal clerks and road repairmen had to pay an average of fifteen to eighteen per cent of the meager salaries on which they supported their families.

In 1947 an Italian industrialist visiting Texas was astonished by the attitude he found there among businessmen who ignored everything Washington did for the state: "They treat your Uncle Sam as if he were a complete stranger. . . . They just want to forget him. It's fantastic!"

Robert W. Calvert, chairman of the Democratic State Executive Committee in Texas, declared in 1947, "The oil industry today is in complete control of the state government and state politics." Ronnie Dugger, contributing editor of the *Texas*

Observer, noted, "The rich think they can buy stock in the legislature or an executive agency as they can in a corporation, and they can." The issue of states' rights was used by oilmen as a façade for anticonsumer operations.

During the Eisenhower administration, the oil lobby succeeded in getting a bill through Congress to remove Federal controls from the price of natural gas, increasing their profits from homeowners by about $1 billion a year. The oilmen insisted that they were simply saving "the industry from the socialist planners in Washington." But President Eisenhower was so shocked by what he denounced as their "arrogant" lobbying that he felt compelled to veto the bill.

The outbreak of the Korean War brought the reimposition of wartime price controls on everything from toasters, irons and frying pans to textiles, clothes and washing machines. Polls showed that eighty-eight per cent of Americans wanted controls kept on and made even stronger. But when President Eisenhower took office he removed them, stating, "We could not live our lives under emergency measures."

Before leaving office President Truman had issued an executive order "setting aside the submerged lands of the Continental Shelf as a naval petroleum reserve." Big business interests, anxious to exploit tidelands oil deposits, pressured the Eisenhower administration into passage of the Tidelands Oil bill, giving states title to submerged lands off their coasts. The Supreme Court upheld the states' rights to tidelands up to three miles offshore (*U.S. v. States of La., Tex., Miss., Ala., and Fla.*, 1960).

Eisenhower, opposed to Federal public power projects like TVA, gave the Idaho Power Company a license to build dams and power stations in Hell's Canyon. Labor groups, the Farmers' Union and consumer groups joined to support Democratic congressmen who fought the license on grounds that the electricity supplied the public would be too high-priced. But the Hell's Canyon project went through under private auspices.

With the arrival of John F. Kennedy at the White House in 1961, the American consumer once more found a sympathetic ear in Washington. In a special message to Congress the President delineated four basic consumer rights—the right to safety; to be informed; to choose; and to be heard.

During the Kennedy and Johnson administrations, consumers

found those rights more than lip service. As a result of medical findings that cigarette smoking led to cancer and heart disease, the tobacco companies were forced to stop advertising on TV and to label cigarette packs with health warnings. A Truth-in-Lending Act compelled finance companies and stores to state clearly in big print how much consumers were being charged for borrowing money or buying merchandise on time. To cut down traffic deaths, Congress passed the National Traffic and Motor Vehicle Safety Act of 1966, setting safety standards for all new cars manufactured. The Highway Safety Act of 1966 also appropriated $267 million on a 50-50 matching basis to the states for the establishment of highway safety programs under a new Department of Transportation.

A growing consumer movement, led by Ralph Nader, compelled many manufacturers to curb deceptive sales practices and shoddy workmanship. Auto companies were forced to recall millions of new cars to correct faults. National advertisers were forced to cancel misleading ads. Farmers were forbidden to spray crops with the poisonous pesticide, DDT.

Many cities followed the example of New York, which in 1967 created a municipal Department of Consumer Affairs to fight deceptive merchandising tactics on the local level.

During the Nixon administration, runaway inflation forced the Government to establish periods of wage and price controls. They worked badly; price ceilings were imposed when prices were already too high; when the controls were removed, most prices continued to rise. The President's economic advisers asked consumers to be patient and wait for abundant supplies of food and other commodities to bring prices down.

In 1969 consumer protests against high gasoline and home heating fuel prices led Nixon to appoint a commission to study the oil quota system, imposed through the influence of the oil lobby to minimize foreign competition. Secretary of Labor George P. Shultz, as commission chairman, found the quota system "no longer acceptable," and reported that scrapping it would save American consumers $5 billion a year.

But President Nixon quietly shelved his own commission's report. Senator William Proxmire of Wisconsin observed, "The consumers have been sacrificed once again to the interests of big oil." *The New York Times* charged that the Nixon administration, which prided itself on "trimming outlays for health, education and welfare, does not mind letting consumers pay out more than $60 billion in extra oil bills over the coming decade." New Englanders were especially angered, since they wanted to import oil directly through a Maine port, eliminating expensive transportation costs for northeastern states.

As a direct result of the sustained oil quota policy, consumers were told by the oil companies in 1973 that there was a chronic oil shortage. Many independent gas stations selling cheaper fuel were forced out of business, as the major companies raised their prices and rationed deliveries. The oil lobby also won passage of the Alaska oil pipeline bill stalled by conservationists.

In September 1973 the attorneys general of all the states met in an angry conference to demand that Congress break up the oil monopoly. Since the Nixon administration had failed to institute Federal antitrust proceedings, six attorneys general announced that they would file suits against the oil companies at the state level. The Connecticut attorney general appealed to all of the states to follow suit.

"We can shake 'em up," he vowed, "then break 'em up!"

The fuel shortage, as noted previously, became a crisis during the Arab-Israeli War. Critics accused the big oil companies of misrepresenting the shortages in order to charge high prices for gas, home heating fuel and oil by-products.

Representative Les Aspin accused the White House of letting the oil companies get away with making huge profits out of public misery because of over $5 million they contributed to the President's reelection campaign in 1972. "After their massive contributions," Aspin said, "there is little he can do to control them."

Both Nixon and his energy czar, William Simon, resisted pressures to introduce gas rationing, preferring to cut down demand by letting the oil companies raise prices. The state of Oregon, however, considered this rationing for the rich at the expense of the poor, and introduced its own rationing system for fair gas distribution to all.

Many garages throughout the nation followed the example of the oil companies by profiteering. Some charged as much as $1 a gallon for gas; others sold gas only to "members" who had to pay $5 for "membership cards." In southern California it was found that over half the service stations were price-gouging. All over the country long lines of cars waited at service stations for hours. There were fights and threats when stations ran out of oil with cars still in line.

The American people were enraged, demanding punishment for the oil companies. The belief persisted that the crisis had been deliberately manufactured. There were calls for heavy taxation of oil profits, and for breaking up oil company monopolies. Senator Henry Jackson prepared a bill to make oil companies public utilities, subject to government supervision and a profit ceiling. Congress took steps to make an independent audit of all U.S. oil reserves because, incredibly, the Government had only the companies' word that a shortage existed!

When the Nixon administration made large-scale sales of wheat to the Soviet Union and Red China, a home shortage sent food prices soaring in 1973. Consumer boycotts of meat erupted across the country, but were only temporarily successful in forcing down prices. A brief period of reimposed Federal price controls also did little to help. American consumers began turning to fish, chicken, eggs and even horsemeat. One group of women stormed into the gallery of the House of Representatives to stage a furious demonstration against the high price of milk.

In August the President signed a farm bill that largely ended farm subsidies and allowed food prices to be set by supply and demand. He saw the bill as eventually stabilizing prices by increasing farm production. Meanwhile prices in the supermarket kept climbing steadily month after month. And in January 1974 bakers warned that a wheat shortage might drive bread to $1 a loaf by the spring.

Throughout this inflationary period, the giant corporations continued to amass record profits, unrestrained by either state or Federal laws. Some 73,000 large corporations have been incorporated in Delaware because of that state's lax regulatory laws. Among them are a third of all companies listed on the New York Stock Exchange and half of the top 100 industrial corporations.

Ralph Nader noted that General Motors, with ninety times Delaware's general revenues, could easily buy the state "if du Pont were willing to sell it." He pointed out, "State incorporation makes as much sense as state currencies. . . . The federal chartering of giant corporations is necessary because state incorporation has failed. Even if state business codes and authorities did not so overwhelmingly reflect management power interests, they are no match for the resources of the great corporations. . . . To control national power requires, at the least, national authority."

Bess Myerson, head of New York City's Department of Consumer Affairs under Mayor Lindsay, complained that the voice of the consumer was still far too weak. "Consumer rights are human rights," she pointed out. ". . . Our marketplace is one of the areas of our national growth where . . . the human rights have yet to be realized. . . . Everyone must buy; no one is neutral. But despite its rapid and widespread growth, the issues of 'consumerism' met resistant or reluctant acknowledgment among many leaders, in business and government."

Some consumers joined together to bring "class action" suits against corporations selling fraudulent, dangerous or faulty products. They sought justice in the courts rather than through Federal regulatory agencies, because the FTC, FDA and FPC often interpreted the law in favor of industries they were supposed to regulate in the public interest.

Pressure by "Nader's Raiders" was influential in getting Congress to pass new laws compelling auto safety, honest drug labeling, truth-in-packaging, safe toys, safer meat inspection standards, and the establishment of a National Commission on Product Safety.

Different consumer trends are in the making, with consumers looking neither to Washington nor Main Street, but to themselves, for protection. Consumer cooperatives are once more springing up in cities across the land to buy groceries and home needs wholesale. Consumer leagues, protection councils and safety commissions are operating to educate consumers and to help those with complaints get satisfaction.

In August 1973 Mrs. Ellen Zawel, president of the new National Consumer Congress, called for a nation-wide consumer strike. "We hope our strike will urge Congress to take long-range steps to break up monopolies and other price-fixing arrangements," she declared. ". . . We want to make business competitive and profits reasonable, not exorbitant. We want products with quality instead of built-in obsolescence. And we want no more wheat deals."

Many Americans who worried about shortages of food, gas and heating oil—and whether they would be able to afford all they needed—were listening.

New Hampshire housewives organized a beef boycott in 1972.

(UNITED PRESS INTERNATIONAL)

15 · Pollution and conservation— whose job?

A secret antipollution crusader who calls himself "The Fox" crawls up an industrial sewage pipe which is spewing sudsy wastes into the Fox River, and clogs the outlet with a plywood bulkhead. He reveals to *Newsweek* reporter Don Holt in 1970 that he is outraged by the poisoning of his favorite fishing stream, a once lovely waterway of Aurora, Ill.

"Nobody ever stuck up for that poor, mistreated stream," he explains, "so I decided to do something in its name."

Not stopping there, The Fox vows a one-man war against the spoliation of the water, air and land around him. Since neither Washington nor Main Street is effectively stopping the corporations responsible, he makes it his own business.

At dusk on another evening, with the aid of a friend, he scales the towering smokestack of a factory belching industrial poisons into the air, and caps it with a homemade metal stopper that forces the fumes back down into the plant.

One night he deposits dead skunks on the front porches of executives who work for companies responsible for the pollution of the Fox River. On another afternoon, wearing work clothes and sunglasses, he enters the reception room of the U.S.

Reduction Co. in East Chicago, which owns an aluminum

"The Fox" waged a one-man war against pollution in Illinois in 1970. (NEWSWEEK)

company in Aurora that pollutes the Fox. He dumps a can containing fifty pounds of raw sewage on the tile floor, sending secretaries fleeing from the horrid smell.

"If we catch The Fox we could charge him with trespassing and criminal damage to property," declares police sergeant Robert Kollwelter. But he admits, "It's kind of hard to lift fingerprints from the inside of a sewer."

"Who's breaking the law, anyway?" The Fox asks *Newsweek*'s Don Holt. "Do you know where I got that raw sewage I dumped at U.S. Reduction? I just went down to the Fox River and took what came out of their pipes." He explains resolutely, "There is a dignity about nature. Man can exploit it but he shouldn't ruin it. I'm trying to stop something that is wrong—and I'm willing to go my own route to do it."

In the eyes of the law he's a fanatical nuisance. But in the view of ecologists, The Fox is an unsung hero who might one day become a romantic legend honored by schoolchildren.

The decay of our environment is a grave problem that concerns all of us personally almost every day. Our surroundings are damaged by industrial smoke and car exhausts, water pollutants, ocean oil spills, mountains of garbage, littered park-

American cities are ringed by junkyards.   (CAROL BASEN)

lands and beaches, deafening jet, truck and motorcycle noise.

At an earlier time in American history, those who failed to cheer on the growth of business and industry were suspect as radicals against "progress." Today many public-minded citizens are fighting tooth and nail to stop such "progress" from polluting the environment of their communities.

The ecology drive has split the country into feuding camps. On one side are conservationists who want more land left in a wild state to keep the balance of nature; a stop to oil drilling (and spills) on the Continental Shelf; an end to corporate pollution of the land, air and water; the use of only product containers that can be recycled; strict curbs on power plants to prevent the destruction of river life.

In opposition are vacationists who want all forest preserves wide open to cars and tourists; sportsmen who want no curbs on their fishing or hunting; realty developers who seek to clear wooded lands; lumber companies that want to harvest trees in state and national forests; mining companies that practice strip mining; and power companies defending pollution as inevitable because of the nation's great need of energy.

Chemicals in the American air cripple Florida cattle, peel paint on Maine homes and cars, kill California pines, ruin orchards in Texas and Illinois. John T. Middleton, commissioner of the National Air Pollution Control Administration, says,

"Americans are paying billions of dollars each year as the price of contaminated air." Worse, increasing numbers of Americans are dying of respiratory ailments—asthma, bronchitis, lung cancer and emphysema.

"Americans are feeling the squeeze," declared former Secretary of the Interior Stewart L. Udall, "in our impacted cities, our choking highways, our disfigured land. We feel it in power failures and water shortages; in smog and sewage and slums. . . . Our rivers and lakes are open sewers; emphysema is claiming lives at an alarming rate; and noise has damaged the hearing of three out of five men. We suicidally abuse our environment—by our numbers, our affluence, our technology."

He warned, "Seventy-eight species of animals are in danger of extinction. . . . Unless we recognize that the earth does not belong to us, but that we belong to it—man may follow the bald eagle into oblivion."

But in 1973 the Nixon administration insisted that the American people would have to tolerate an even higher level of pollution in the future, because of severe shortages of oil and other fuels to supply all of their energy needs. And citizens of towns with a high rate of ill health because of polluting industries resisted Federal regulation, fearing it would force plants to shut down and throw them out of work.

More and more we are being compelled to face the crucial question of the future—how much are we willing to sacrifice of our standard of living . . . our cars, air conditioners, fully heated homes, millions of plastic products . . . in order to keep the air, water and land around us livable?

Private profit has long had primary consideration over the public welfare in matters of conservation and pollution. The Mining Law of 1872, still operative today, permitted individuals or companies to search for minerals on Federal lands by cutting roads through timber, as well as bulldozing and dredging or stripping land at will. Great cliffs of mine wastes blew into adjacent towns, polluting their air and streams.

During most of the nineteenth century neither Washington nor Main Street displayed much concern about conservation because of the nation's great wealth of natural resources. Not until 1890 did conservationists like Gifford Pinchot and Theodore Roosevelt

Acres of land are laid bare by mining operations.

(G. BRIMACOMBE, BLACK STAR)

begin to make Americans aware of the need for the Federal government to act swiftly in order to preserve the ecological balance of earth, water, plants and animals.

The following year Congress passed the Forest Reserve Act establishing our system of national forests, and in 1892 the National Reclamation (Newlands) Act authorized the use of funds from public land sales in the West to finance irrigation projects in the arid states. Through this Act over seven million wasteland acres were reclaimed in seventeen states.

During the Roosevelt administration, however, a scandal erupted when Department of Interior officials were found to have accepted bribes to permit the exploitation of public lands by timber thieves, mine-jumpers and crooked realtors. Main Street was in no position to point a finger because many state legislatures also squandered state resources of water, forest and soil by handing them over to private predators.

"We are prone to speak of the resources of this country as inexhaustible," Roosevelt warned Congress; "this is not so. . . .

Wastefulness in dealing with it today means that our descendants will feel the exhaustion."

But that same year a western grazing lobby succeeded in getting the Forest Reserve Act repealed. And when the First National Conservation Congress convened in Seattle the following year, it was controlled by the lumber interests.

In 1918 the United States and Canada signed a Migratory Bird Treaty to protect such flocks from being hunted into extinction. Sportsmen in Missouri attacked the treaty as unconstitutional because it violated the Tenth Amendment, infringing on "powers reserved to the states and the people." But in 1920 Supreme Court Justice Oliver Wendell Holmes ruled that the powers of the Federal government were almost limitless when written into an international treaty.

That year Congress passed a Mineral Leasing Act regulating the exploitation of minerals in public lands. But the oil lobby rejoiced when President Warren Harding appointed as Secretary of the Interior Albert Fall, who had publicly called for transferring public lands to private hands. Fall secretly leased the Government's oil reserve at Teapot Dome, Wyoming, to oilman Harry Sinclair for a $100,000 bribe. When a newsman dug up the story in 1923, Fall was forced to resign in a scandal that discredited the Harding administration.

Entering the White House in 1933, Franklin D. Roosevelt called for large-scale development of public power projects, telling Americans, "I promise you this: Never shall the Federal Government part with its sovereignty or with its control over its power resources, while I am President of the United States." He sponsored public power projects that produced twenty per cent of the nation's electricity needs. The Tennessee Valley Authority (TVA) built multipurpose dams which served as reservoirs to control floods, while generating cheap, abundant hydroelectric power.

TVA also manufactured fertilizer, dug navigation channels, undertook soil conservation and reforestation, and cooperated with state and local agencies in a vast regional experiment of social planning. It won enthusiastic support from almost four million people in seven states to whom it brought electricity and light at rates far below those of private utilities. Cheap power also helped attract industry, raising the low living standards of the Valley.

Representative Joe Martin of Massachusetts attacked TVA as "patterned closely after one of the Soviet dreams." Private utilities challenged Washington's right to compete with them locally. But the Supreme Court ruled in 1936 that the dams built by TVA were a legitimate exercise of the Federal government's right to control navigable streams and provide for adequate national defense (*Ashwander v. TVA*).

For many years public lands were grazed by cattle raisers without restraints. In 1934 the New Deal passed the Taylor Grazing Act setting aside eight million acres—later raised to 142 million—for grazing purposes, but under the supervision and licensing of the Interior Department. One objective was to keep the lands from being exploited by mining companies. In 1935 Roosevelt set aside the remainder of public lands in the nation for purposes of conservation.

According to an 1845 Supreme Court decision, "The shores of navigable water, and the soils under them, were not granted by the Constitution to the United States, but were reserved to the States respectively." Nevertheless in September 1945 President Harry S. Truman, by executive order, asserted Federal jurisdiction over all natural resources of the entire Continental Shelf. California challenged this claim.

In 1947 the Supreme Court ruled that while Washington did not own the states' offshore lands, it did have "paramount rights in and power over them," to protect the nation's coast and to regulate international commerce (*United States v. California*). The oil lobby pressured Congress for a "states' rights" bill that would give individual states the right to lease their own tidelands.

"It's not a matter of states' rights," charged former Secretary of the Interior Harold L. Ickes, "but the issue of the rights of certain oil companies to take oil from the states because it's easier. Those who are backing bills to continue state ownership are raising the cry 'Stop thief' in order to let the oil companies get away with murder."

After Truman's election victory in 1948, Attorney General Tom Clark filed a Federal suit against Louisiana and Texas to stop those states from "trespassing" on offshore tidelands. The

Supreme Court again upheld the Government. Congressman Gossett of Texas cried, "The Supreme Court has given the nation another long shove down the road to national socialism!" The Texas state land commissioner refused to turn over to Washington over $8 million in oil lease receipts.

Soon after Eisenhower's inauguration in 1953, Congress passed the Submerged Lands Act restoring the tidelands to the states. The President signed it into law declaring, "I deplore and I will always resist Federal encroachment upon rights and affairs of the states." To silence the protests of those who charged a sellout to the oil lobby, Washington was allowed to retain title to lands on the outer Continental Shelf beyond the three-mile limit.

In a test case, the constitutionality of the new Act was upheld by the Supreme Court (*Alabama v. Texas*, 1954). The Court also ruled in 1960 that Texas and Florida had jurisdiction over ten and a half adjacent miles of Mexican Gulf waters. Texas Governor Price Daniels jubilantly appointed his successful lawyers admirals in the "Texas Navy."

The air pollution problem was dramatized in 1948 when stagnant air, fog and factory fumes combined to blanket the small industrial town of Donora, Pennsylvania, in a thick black smog. Before the air was cleared by wind and rain four days later, twenty people had died, and almost half the townspeople complained of coughs, sore throats, difficult breathing, irritated eyes, nausea and vomiting. Other industrial cities began banning the use of high-pollution fuels in homes and factories.

The U.S. Public Health Service estimated that over 100 million Americans lived in cities with an air pollution problem, and for half of those it had reached major proportions. In 1955 the U.S. Health Service began assisting state and local governments in air pollution control.

One year later Congress passed a Federal Water Pollution Control Act under which, for the first time, Washington furnished funds for the construction of municipal waste treatment facilities, research and pure water enforcement.

The American public became aware of a new threat to the environment and public health from the use of pesticides in 1962, when Rachel Carson published her book, *Silent Spring*. She warned that the use of DDT was killing fish, birds and insects in massive numbers, seriously disturbing Nature's ecological balance and slowly poisoning humans as well. Her disclosures eventually led to a Federal ban on the use of DDT.

Many states were reluctant to enforce air pollution control programs because of the expense involved. Congress consequently passed the first Clean Air Act in 1963, increasing Federal financial and technical assistance to state and local pollution control agencies.

Pressure for a stronger Federal role in water purification came in 1963 with the U.S. Surgeon General's report that over thirty million Americans lived in 1,500 communities which permitted either sewage or factory wastes to be discharged into the streams from which they drew their drinking water.

The Clean Air Act of 1963 added Federal support to state and local pollution-control agencies.

(CAROL BASEN)

State water laws were highly ineffectual, and state funds to help local communities control water pollution were negligible. In one-third of the states, not a single polluter had been brought to court between 1956 and 1961. The chief problem was the states' fear of driving away industries guilty of polluting streams. In 1961 Congress amended the Water Pollution Control Act to strengthen its enforcement provisions.

Proposing his "Great Society" in May 1964, President Lyndon B. Johnson declared, "The water we drink, the food we eat, the very air that we breathe, are threatened with pollution. Our parks are overcrowded, our seashores overburdened. Green fields and dense forests are disappearing." He promised Federal programs to tackle all these problems.

One result was the Wilderness Act of 1964, placing over nine million acres of Government land into a wilderness conservation system, with car travel and commercial establishments banned. But conservationists fought administration plans to divert water from rivers of the Northwest to irrigate the water-poor Southwest. Additional dams and waterworks, they charged, would impair the natural beauty of the canyons. Northern California and adjacent states also opposed them out of fear of depleted water supplies, charging "unwarranted interference with states' rights and resources."

Through the active support of Mrs. Lady Bird Johnson, the First Lady, Congress was induced in 1965 to pass a "Highway Beautification" bill to end the spoiling of landscaping on Federal highways by outdoor billboards and junkyards.

In that year Congress also passed legislation giving states and communities aid in developing solid waste disposal systems to cut down river pollution. But the problem persisted because over 5,000 industries, lacking treatment plants for their own waste disposal, continued to dump raw industrial sewage into the rivers.

On Thanksgiving Day, 1966, polluted air trapped above New York City killed 168 people, once again emphasizing the urgent need to purify the air over America's cities. Passage of a 1967 Clean Air Act and public hearings in many states brought tough new smokestack standards for industry.

In 1969 offshore oil rigs were ordered to stop drilling operations by the Department of Interior when one near Santa Barbara began spilling oil uncontrollably, fouling forty miles of

The Santa Barbara oil slick fouled forty miles of California coast in 1969.
(UNITED PRESS INTERNATIONAL)

Southern California beaches, destroying sea life, killing sea birds and soiling thousands of small boats.

By 1970 the whole issue of pollution had so aroused the American people that Washington and Main Street were both hearing from them in no uncertain terms. When the town fathers of Trenton, Maine, sought approval for the building of a nuclear power plant and an aluminum factory, Trenton citizens voted a loud "No!" by 144 to 77, despite their need of the added jobs and tax relief the new industry would bring.

When Florida's legislature sought to build a jetport near the Everglades, infuriated conservationists forced the Federal government to stop its construction, on grounds that the noise would imperil flora and fauna in the national park.

Public concern compelled thirteen Congressional committees to study environmental problems. Congress voted ninety separate antipollution programs. But the crisis grew even faster.

Senator Gaylord Nelson of Wisconsin warned in 1970, "Progress—American style—adds up each year to 200 million tons of smoke and fumes, seven million junked cars, twenty million tons of paper, forty-eight billion cans and twenty-eight billion bottles."

A nonprofit youth organization, Environmental Action, Inc., organized "Earth Day" on April 22, 1970, to dramatize the perils of pollution. The White House did not participate, but over twenty-two United States senators did, along with many governors. Over 2,000 college campuses, 2,000 community groups and 10,000 schools joined in nation-wide demonstrations. Volunteers helped clean up littered ghettos; car engines were buried in mock funerals; students wore gas masks to protest air pollution; young people collected trash for return to the companies that produced it.

The antilitter campaign spread. Washington State passed a law requiring all drivers to carry litter bags. Richland County, South Carolina, punished litterers with a forty-hour sentence to pick up garbage along highways. After a Connecticut family had been allowed to camp on a western ranch near Big Horn, Wyoming, the rancher noted that they had kept the camping area clean by

Earth Day, April 22, 1970.   (WIDE WORLD PHOTOS)

throwing their trash over a fence onto a neighbor's property. Collecting it, he wrapped it neatly and returned it to them by mail.

In 1970 Congress responded to public pressure by establishing a new Federal Environmental Protection Agency (EPA), with the power to establish national air quality standards necessary to protect public health. The EPA cooperated with state and local governments, and with industry.

Each state was required to hold a public hearing, then prepare a plan to achieve Federal air quality standards for EPA approval. The states had up to five years to reach that goal, unless special circumstances required an extension of time. Minimum pollution auto systems were ordered by 1975.

The EPA could obtain a court order to shut down any polluters when pollution in the area became a health threat. It could also take over enforcement in any state that tolerated widespread violations. In November 1971 when Birmingham, Alabama, suffered a serious air pollution crisis, county health officials asked twenty-three major industries to cut back production.

The major polluters refused. EPA obtained a court order compelling all twenty-three plants to stop or reduce production until the stagnant air mass cleared away. This act alarmed some city councils and state legislatures, which expressed fear that EPA might even call out National Guardsmen to keep cars out of cities and cabs off streets to control pollution.

But EPA general counsel John Quarles assured them, "We don't really believe these plans can be enforced without coopera- tion from state and city officials, and we're truly anxious to get that cooperation."

Richard Ayers of the National Resources Defense Council acknowledged, "The Clear Air Act says if the state conks out, the feds are supposed to take over the program and run it. Sure there is a knotty Constitutional problem in how far you can go in usurping state power, but I don't think it's that knotty. . . . EPA doesn't have the armies and it doesn't have the guts to ask for them, and it probably couldn't get them if it did. This Adminis- tration doesn't want to tangle with the states."

In highly industrialized cities like Gary, Indiana, the air is so polluted that homeowners have to paint their homes once a year; new cars age quickly due to corrosion; beaches and fishing holes have been ruined; and visibility is often only a few feet. But steelworkers who made $5.50 an hour in 1970 were unwilling to swap clean air for unemployment. So in Gary sulphuric acid in rainwater continues to char lawns brown, eat holes in leaves, and strip birds of feathers.

Gary is not unique. Acidic wastes from factories have killed Lake Erie, destroyed the brown pelicans of Louisiana, and scarred Cleopatra's Needle, the rare 3,000-year-old Eygptian obelisk brought to New York in 1881.

In Los Angeles, a Clean Air Council organized a boycott against the purchase of new cars, posting pickets in front of General Motors dealers with signs reading "Lung Decay by Chevrolet" and "Smog—Think Before You Buy." In Chicago, consumers organized a campaign to stop paying bills to Commonwealth Edison until its smokestacks stopped fouling the city.

The Department of Justice, pressured by public indignation, brought charges against twenty New York and New Jersey firms for polluting the waters of New York Harbor; against Florida Light and Power Co. for fouling Biscayne Bay; against the Reserve Mining Company for dumping tailings in Lake Superior. Four states—Illinois, Indiana, Michigan and Wisconsin—were ordered to enforce a ban against dumping wastes into Lake Michigan by all industries within their borders.

In 1971 the Ford Motor Company was fined $10,000 for shipping cars to dealers before the cars were certified as meeting emission standards. The fine jumped to $7 million in 1973 for violating Federal test requirements.

On the other hand, fear of Americans that they would not have enough gas for their cars and oil heat for their homes led Congress to reject ecological arguments against the building of an oil pipeline across the Alaska tundra. The victory of the oil lobby at the end of 1973 led conservationists to accuse the lobby of winning the pipeline the oilmen wanted by a scare campaign about oil shortages.

Ecology-minded Americans were also dismayed at how quickly, once the energy scare had been raised, both Washington and Main Street yielded to big business pressures to relax antipollution regulations. Power companies and big plants were once more permitted to burn sulphurous coal. New areas of coal deposits were opened up to strip mining. Once again preparations were made to drill for oil off American beaches, even in nature preserves. The deadline for antipollution on cars was postponed.

Minor battles have been won in the fight against noise pollution. Los Angeles International Airport was compelled to ban almost all take-offs and landings over populated areas between 11:00 P.M. and 6:00 A.M. New York City fined drivers $50 for any unnecessary horn honking. Chicago imposed decibel limits on jackhammers, air conditioners, sirens and garbage trucks. In July 1972 Congress passed a Noise Control Act under which the Environmental Protection Agency moved to curb noise levels from interstate trucks and busses and to require modified, quieter engines for jet planes.

In August 1973 Colorado authorities were horrified to discover that in the town of Grand Junction, landfill used for construction and taken from an atomic energy test site after being certified safe by the Atomic Energy Commission, was dangerously radioactive. The town's homeowners and schoolchildren were threatened with cancer. A quarrel ensued between Federal and state authorities as to which was responsible for digging up and replacing the radioactive dirt. Washington finally agreed to appropriate $5 million for the project, with the state providing $600,000.

The task of halting the deterioration of our environment is more enormous now than ever, primarily because the energy shortage has given our major polluters the opportunity to erase many of the gains conservationists had worked so hard to win over the years. Americans who are worried about enough gas for their cars, enough fuel for their homes, enough electricity for their lights, TV and air conditioners, and enough power to keep their places of employment open, are going to permit big business to resume polluting the environment if they are convinced the choice is between pollution and energy shortages.

From the record, Main Street will not put up a very strong fight against the powerful corporations. The question is whether Congress or the White House can determine the whole truth about the energy crisis and is willing to protect the American people by refusing to relax antipollution regulations one scintilla more than is absolutely necessary.

16 · Power to the people

A strong use of presidential powers lifted the nation out of the terrible Depression of the Thirties. But it also plunged the nation into the shock of the Watergate scandal of the Seventies, when the Nixon administration committed illegal acts to stay in office and enlarge its powers.

The American people were sobered into the realization that big government could swiftly degenerate into Big-Brother-Is-Watching-You government. Power tends to corrupt, as Lord Acton said, and absolute power tends to corrupt absolutely.

Writing twenty-two years before Watergate, E. H. Carr declared in his book, *The New Society*, "The spectacle of an efficient elite maintaining its authority and asserting its will over the mass by . . . irrational methods of persuasion is the most disturbing nightmare of mass democracy."

But there are equal dangers in shifting the balance of power to Main Street. State legislatures and city halls were given greater control over the operation of schools, police, zoning, real estate developments, welfare programs and urban rehabilitation under Nixon's revenue-sharing "New Federalism."

This program had great appeal for his "silent majority," who under the Democrats had felt too small and powerless to protest Federal programs that seemed to benefit underprivileged minorities at the expense of the lower middle class.

"The champions of revenue sharing say it will bring government closer to the people, make it more responsive," observed Professor Amitai Etzioni, Director of the Center for Policy Research. "But it might well bring it closer to the control of the local establishments, which are often less responsive to 'the people,' *all* the people, than is Washington."

That, in effect, is what happened. C. David Loeks, president of the Mid-Hudson Pattern For Progress of upstate New York, acknowledged, "People are beginning to question the capability of local government to provide services and guide growth and development in an orderly, efficient, economical fashion."

It is no secret that corruption is commonplace in city halls and state capitals. By 1971 in New Jersey, for example, Herbert J. Stern, a new and honest U.S. District Attorney, had brought no less than sixty-one high city and state officials to trial for bribery, conspiracy, extortion, tax evasion, mail fraud and perjury. "The same things are going on in other states," Stern declared. "They just don't get caught."

A Ford Foundation study found many legislatures to be inept, understaffed, poorly paid, in "disarray," and dominated by their governors. Governors often accept kickbacks, disguised as campaign contributions, from businessmen in return for state contracts awarded without competitive bidding.

This was the accusation leveled against Vice President Spiro Agnew in 1973 by a group of Baltimore contractors, covering the period he was governor of Maryland and even after he became Vice President. Agnew was convicted of tax evasion, fined and compelled to resign as Vice President. Governors also often make deals with political bosses, giving them patronage—control of jobs and government contracts—in return for votes.

"You can't keep an organization together without patronage," explained Matthew Troy, a New York political boss. "Men ain't in politics for nothing. They want to get something out of it. . . . With Rockefeller, the state patronage I get is all part of deals, usually for votes he needs in the Legislature."

A *Nation* editorial observed, "A possible weakness in . . . returning power to the people is that state and city corruption is at least one order of magnitude greater than federal corruption. By way of example, federal judges do not as a rule buy their offices or accept bribes from litigants, but such procedures are almost routine in the lower levels of government."

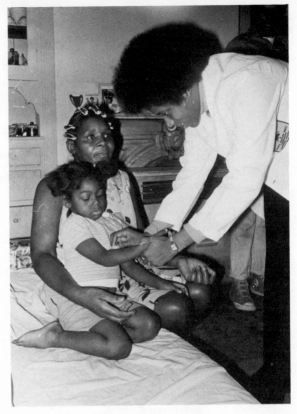

In some cities black and other ethnic groups have set up their own community-action programs. Here a Black Panther health worker tests a child for sickle-cell anemia.
(S. SHAMES, BLACK STAR)

Most Americans are suspicious of state legislatures, characterizing them, according to reporter Bernard McCormick, as "a bunch of thieves." In April 1973 a Rutgers University survey found that three out of four Americans polled believed that their local government was corrupt or partly corrupt.

"I have no hesitation in stating my deep conviction," declared Senator Joseph S. Clark of Pennsylvania, a former mayor of Philadelphia, in 1965, "that the legislatures of America . . . are presently the greatest menace in our country to the successful operation of the democratic process."

Taking the Nixon administration at its word that it sought greater self-government by Main Street, blacks and other ethnic groups began demanding more power in their own communities. Some worried Americans saw stronger local government as leading to less, not more, democracy.

"If the unit of government becomes the neighborhood," warned Harvard Professor James Q. Wilson, ". . . the opportunities for a small, self-serving minority to seize control of the police or the schools will become very great indeed."

Richard E. Rubenstein, Assistant Director of the Adlai Stevenson Institute, agreed that "strong local government under conditions of political somnolence means that power will be grabbed by those piratical enough to grab it and utilized by those ruthless enough to utilize it."

Much depends on whether "power to the people" at the local level falls into honest, democratic hands, or into the grasp of unscrupulous politicians. In the period from 1880 to 1930 most cities were run by political bosses who manipulated masses of immigrants by exchanging favors for votes.

On the other hand, in the early period after Jefferson, enlightened state legislatures and town meetings ended property qualifications for voting and established state universities. In the early 1900s progressive and Socialist mayors initiated modern city planning and "good government" programs.

"Under certain circumstances," Rubenstein asserts, "maximizing human freedom may require that the central government assume vast new powers in order to counter-balance increased private power; in others it will require that oppressed and alienated communities become self-determining."

Advocates of strong self-government for cities and towns in which blacks and other ethnic minorities now form a majority believe that such government close to the people is in the best democratic tradition of New England town meetings.

It was not the cities or states, however, but the Federal government which gave Americans the health, education, welfare, labor, civil rights, urban renewal, transportation, housing, farm and conservation programs they enjoy today. The states have often attempted to seize control of these programs for political purposes and patronage.

Justice Oliver Wendell Holmes once observed that it would be no great tragedy if the Supreme Court lost the power to overturn acts of Congress, but, "I do think the Union would be imperiled if we could not make that declaration as to the laws of the several States."

The philosophy of states' rights is a respectable one, with much to recommend it. Too often, however, it has been discredited by its use as a cloak to nullify the decisions of the Federal government. Lobbyists for powerful financial interests prefer weak Federal and strong state governments, because they can

A modern-day New England town meeting.
(KOSTI RUOHOMAA, BLACK STAR)

push their bills through more easily and cheaply at the state and local levels. Such lobbies erode good government both in Washington and Main Street.

State legislatures tend to meet too infrequently and briefly, because many legislators are lawyers busy with private practices. Often in their haste to adjourn, they rush through bills by voice vote—bills they have scarcely read, let alone studied. Many of these bills are written for legislators by lobbyists. "It is common for a special interest to be the only source of legislative information about itself," observed California politician Jesse Unruh.

Philadelphia reporter Bernard McCormick noted that in the Pennsylvania legislature, the Sun Oil lobbyist "is often referred to as the 51st senator," and the lobbyist for Penn Central "is considered the 52nd."

In 1970 Richard W. Cardwell, counsel for the Hoosier State Press Association, published a study of the fifty state legislatures which reported, "Many state legislatures continue to . . . conduct, in committee, much of the public's business in secret . . . closed-door decision making."

On the other hand it is sometimes Washington which rides roughshod over the public interest at the behest of powerful lobbies. In 1973 Congress indicated its readiness to pass a Nixon administration bill empowering the Federal government to build new superports to accommodate oil supertankers in any coastal state, whether or not the state wanted one.

Governor William T. Cahill of New Jersey, a state heavily dependent upon its beach resort industry, denounced the bill as "an environmental nightmare." Senator Harrison A. Williams of New Jersey pressed his own bill to grant the states veto power over superport construction. "States which face this type of threat," he insisted, "should have power to control any potential offshore development which could result in contamination of the ocean and beachfront."

If Washington frequently denies freedom of choice to Main Street in matters affecting the economy, Main Street often sabotages Washington's laws supporting the Bill of Rights.

"It is the states that interfere most frequently with academic freedom," observes Commager, "the states that set up censorship . . . the states that threaten freedom of association . . . the states that have most frequently flouted the due process of law and denied equal protection of the laws, and challenged or denied religious freedom."

Arthur Krock, former Washington Bureau chief for *The New York Times*, thinks, however, that Supreme Court decisions have sharply reduced state sovereignty. He foresees a time in the future when state borders will melt away, to be replaced by new regions whose boundaries will be fixed by common economic and sociologic interests.

A move in this direction has been attempted by New York, New Jersey and Connecticut, which have organized a Tri-State Transportation Committee to experiment with new commuter services that would enable commuters to park outside central business districts of cities, and be sped to their jobs by efficient urban transportation systems. Washington is helping such regional experiments with grants-in-aid.

Despite basic weaknesses in government at the state level, some legislatures do a better job than others. A Citizens Conference on State Legislatures recently made a study of all fifty states and evaluated them in order of excellence.

At the top of the list were (1) California, (2) New York, (3) Illinois, (4) Florida, (5) Wisconsin, (6) Iowa, (7) Hawaii, (8) Michigan, (9) Nebraska and (10) Minnesota. The ten worst, in order, were (1) Alabama, (2) Wyoming, (3) Delaware, (4) North Carolina, (5) Arkansas, (6) Georgia, (7) South Carolina, (8) Arizona, (9) Mississippi and (10) Montana.

"Instead of being 'closer to the people,'" observed Maxwell S. Stewart, secretary of the Public Affairs Committee, "state and local governments often seem to be controlled by cliques and factions that are insensitive to the needs of their poorer residents. Experience seems to show that some disadvantaged people—children, the aged, disabled, blind, and other handicapped persons—arouse sufficient national sympathy and support for Congress to vote funds for their specific needs. But in state houses and city halls these same groups cannot compete with vested interests like the road-building or tax lobbies."

Most Americans agree that the welfare programs of most states and cities are a "mess." Sooner or later Congress will probably adopt some version of President Nixon's plan for a "guaranteed annual wage," which will not permit any American family's income to fall below a certain annual minimum. This Federal solution to the problem would end state and city inequalities and relieve unfair financial burdens on local governments, while making it possible for those receiving the minimum wage to add to it by taking jobs.

Recognizing that our system of law enforcement is also badly in need of overhauling, the Center for the Study of Democratic Institutions has raised some questions Americans will have to decide in the near future: "Do we really need over forty thousand Federal, state and local forces? To what size of police unit should we be aiming in different parts of the country? Should local communities still run their own jails, or would it not be preferable to aim toward a state-wide regionalized prison and jail system?"

After the use of troops during the turbulent sixties in such tragedies as Kent State and Jackson State, we may expect future administrations to rely less upon committing soldiers against civilians, and more on the use of well-trained local and state police. Most Americans now believe that the National Guard and Federal troops should be called in to handle civilian disorders only as a last resort.

Perhaps the rights of the individual can be better protected on the one hand against Federal encroachment, and on the other against Main Street corruption or bigotry, by borrowing from the Scandinavians their system of the ombudsman, which has worked very well for the Swedes for 165 years.

Congressman Henry Reuss of Wisconsin has suggested that teams of people be trained for a Federal ombudsman office that would investigate all complaints now pouring into congressmen's offices and correct injustices brought to light. Congressman Les Aspin of Wisconsin has proposed that one ombudsman be elected for each local Congressional district.

An ombudsman system would go far toward lessening the alienation of many citizens who now feel isolated from the processes of government, being convinced that both Washington and Main Street are deaf to their problems. It would permit every citizen to challenge arbitrary treatment by any government bureaucrat—Federal, state or local—confident that he will not get a "run-around," or have his complaint bogged down in endless red tape.

The Scandinavians have found that the mere existence of the ombudsman system exercises a preventive influence that cuts down arrogance, inefficiency, mistakes and corruption on the part of officeholders and public servants, who are aware of their accountability to the ombudsman. All it takes to start an investigation is a simple letter to the ombudsman's office, giving the facts of a complaint.

In Norway about one in five complaints is found to be justified, and in these cases swift and full justice is done the citizen's cause. In addition to a Federal ombudsman's office, Norway has added special ombudsmen to handle county and municipal problems directly. New Zealand, which also uses the ombudsman system, reports that in 1972 out of 1,248 complaints received from its small population, twenty-eight per cent were verified as valid and rectified.

Whether there is misgovernment by Washington or Main Street, it is too easy to blame political leaders for it. Those leaders did not get in power without the votes of the American people who believed in and supported them. Lincoln Steffens once reminded us, "The misgovernment of the American people is misgovernment *by* the American people."

Representatives who misgovern us are *our* representatives. Perhaps it is not just a question of "throwing the rascals out and electing a new bunch," but of insisting upon political candidates of the highest integrity, instead of those picked by political bosses, or who obviously represent the interests of rich and powerful lobbies.

Undoubtedly the conflict over whether we should be governed more by Washington or Main Street will continue to seesaw back and forth for generations to come. No one solution can satisfy everyone for long. There are advantages and disadvantages to both. We need to strengthen Federal government where it functions best, and local government where it can satisfy our needs better than remote Washington.

In the final analysis, you and millions of your own generation will eventually swing the seesaw between Washington and Main Street up or down in the way most of you decide that your own special times require.

Bibliography and Suggested Further Reading

(° Indicates recommended reading)

° Acheson, Patricia C. *The Supreme Court*. New York: Dodd, Mead & Company, 1961.

Adler, Bill, ed. *Washington: A Reader*. New York: Meredith Press, 1967.

Adler, Renata. *Toward A Radical Middle*. New York: Random House, 1969.

Alsop, Stewart. *The Center*. New York, Evanston, and London: Harper & Row, Publishers, 1967.

Archer, Jules. *The Extremists*. New York: Hawthorn Books, Inc., Publishers, 1969.

————. *Hawks, Doves and the Eagle*. New York: Hawthorn Books, Inc., Publishers, 1970.

————. *Indian Foe, Indian Friend*. New York and London: Crowell-Collier Press, 1970.

° ————. *Laws That Changed America*. New York: Criterion Books, 1967.

————. *Resistance*. Philadelphia: Macrae Smith Company, 1973.

Baker, Leonard. *The Johnson Eclipse*. New York: The Macmillan Company, 1966.

Bainbridge, John. *The Super-Americans*. Garden City, New York: Doubleday & Company, Inc., 1961. (On Texans.)

Baum, B. H. *Decentralization of Authority In a Bureaucracy*. Englewood Cliffs, N.J.: Prentice-Hall, Inc., 1961.

Berman, Harold J., ed. *Talks On American Law*. New York: Vintage Books, 1961.

Blumberg, Abraham S. *The Scales of Justice.* Chicago: Aldine Publishing Co., 1970.

Boorstin, Daniel J., ed. *An American Primer.* New York and Toronto: The New American Library, 1968.

Brower, Brock. *Other Loyalties.* New York: Atheneum, 1968. (On civil liberties.)

° Burns, John. *The Sometime Governments.* New York, Toronto and London: Bantam Books, 1971. (On state legislatures.)

° Cater, Douglass. *Power In Washington.* New York: Vintage Books, 1964.

Chute, William J., ed. *The American Scene: 1600–1860.* New York, Toronto and London: Bantam Books, 1964.

——— . *The American Scene: 1860 to the Present.* New York, Toronto and London: Bantam Books, 1966.

Clark, Ramsey. *Crime In America.* New York: Simon and Schuster, 1970.

° Commager, Henry Steele. *Freedom and Order.* Cleveland and New York: The World Publishing Company, 1966.

° Conkin, Paul K. *FDR and the Origins of the Welfare State.* New York: Thomas Y. Crowell Company, 1967.

Cranston, Ruth. *The Story of Woodrow Wilson.* New York: Simon and Schuster, 1945.

° De Bell, Carrett, ed. *The Environmental Handbook.* New York: Ballantine Books, Inc., 1970.

° Dorman, Michael. *Under 21.* New York: Dell Publishing Co., Inc., 1970.

° Douglas, William O. *The Right of the People.* New York: Arena Books, 1972.

Eisenhower, Dwight D. *Mandate For Change.* New York: The New American Library, 1965.

——— . *Waging Peace.* Garden City, New York: Doubleday & Company, Inc., 1965.

° Ekirch, Arthur A., Jr. *The Civilian and the Military.* New York: Oxford University Press, 1956.

Epstein, Jason. *The Great Conspiracy Trial.* New York: Random House, 1970. (On the Chicago Seven trial.)

Facts about Norway. Oslo: Chr. Schibsteds Forlag, 1970.

Facts about Denmark. Copenhagen: Politikens Forlag, 1969.

Facts about Sweden. Forum: The Swedish Institute, 1969.

Forster, Arnold, and Benjamin R. Epstein. *Danger On the Right.* New York: Random House, 1964.

° Frost, Richard. *Cases In State and Local Government.* Englewood Cliffs, N.J.: Prentice-Hall, Inc., 1951.

Gertz, Elmer. *Moment of Madness*. Chicago, New York: Follett Publishing Company, 1968. (On the assassination of Oswald by Ruby.)

Ginzburg, Ralph, and Warren Boroson. *The Best of* Fact. New York: Avant-Garde Books, 1967. (On welfare and civil liberties.)

Goldman, Eric F. *The Tragedy of Lyndon Johnson*. London: Macdonald and Company (Publishers) Ltd., 1969.

° Goldwin, Robert A. *A Nation of States*. Chicago: Rand McNally & Company, 1968.

° Grant, Joanne, ed. *Black Protest*. Greenwich, Conn: Fawcett Publications, Inc., 1968.

° Graves, W. Brooke. *American Governmental Relations*. New York: Charles Scribner's Sons, 1964.

° Green, Mark J., James M. Fallows, David R. Zwick. *Who Runs Congress?* Toronto, New York, London: Bantam Books, 1972.

Gunther, John. *Inside U.S.A.* New York: Bantam Books, 142.

° Heffner, Richard D. *A Documentary History of the United States*. New York: The New American Library, 1952.

Hofstadter, Richard. *Great Issues In American History: 1765–1865*. New York: Vintage Books, 1958.

——— . *Great Issues In American History: 1864–1969*. New York: Vintage Books, 1969.

° Hyman, Sidney. *The Politics of Consensus*. New York: Random House, 1968.

Janeway, Eliot. *The Economics of Crisis*. New York: Weybright and Talley, 1968.

Johnson, Lyndon Baines. *The Vantage Point*. New York: Popular Library, 1971.

Krock, Arthur. *In the Nation: 1932–1966*. New York, Toronto, London, Sydney: McGraw-Hill Book Company, 1966.

° ——— . *The Consent of the Governed*. Boston, Toronto: Little, Brown and Company, 1971.

° Leach, Richard H. *American Federalism*. New York: W. W. Norton & Company, Inc., 1970.

° Leinwand, Gerald, ed. *Civil Rights and Civil Liberties*. New York: Washington Square Press, Inc., 1968.

° Letwin, William, ed. *A Documentary History of American Economic Policy Since 1789*. Chicago: Aldine Publishing Company, 1961.

° Leuchtenburg, William E. *Franklin D. Roosevelt and the New Deal*. New York: Harper & Row, Publishers, 1963.

° Lindsay, John V. *The City*. New York: The New American Library, 1970.

Lippmann, Walter. *Early Writings*. New York: Liveright, 1970.

Lukas, J. Anthony. *The Barnyard Epithet and Other Obscenities.* New York, Evanston, and London: Harper & Row, Publishers, 1970. (On the Chicago Seven trial.)

° Madison, Charles A. *Leaders and Liberals in 20th Century America.* New York: Frederick Ungar Publishing Co., 1961.

° Marden, Charles F. *Minorities in American Society.* New York, Cincinnati, Chicago, Boston, Atlanta, Dallas, San Francisco: American Book Company, 1952.

° Markmann, Charles Lam. *The Noblest Cry.* New York: St. Martin's Press, 1965. (On civil liberties.)

° McCord, John H., ed. *With All Deliberate Speed.* Urbana, Chicago, London: University of Illinois Press, 1969. (On civil rights.)

Merrill, Walter M. *Against Wind and Tide.* Cambridge, Massachusetts: Harvard University Press, 1963. (On abolition.)

Meyer, Karl E., ed. *Senator Fulbright.* New York: Macfadden Books, 1964.

Miles, Michael W. *The Radical Probe.* New York: Atheneum, 1971.

Miller, Douglas T. *Jacksonian Democracy.* New York: Oxford University Press, 1967.

° Mintz, Morton, and Jerry S. Cohen. *America, Inc.* New York: Dell Publishing Co., Inc., 1972. (On big business influence.)

° *Mississippi Black Paper.* New York: Random House, 1965.

° Mitau, G. Theodore. *Decade of Decision.* New York: Charles Scribner's Sons, 1967. (On the Warren Court.)

° ———. *State and Local Government Politics and Processes.* New York: Charles Scribner's Sons, 1966.

Mitgang, Herbert. *America at Random.* New York: Coward-McCann, Inc., 1969.

Mollenhoff, Clark R. *The Pentagon.* New York: G. P. Putnam's Sons, 1967.

Morris, Joe Alex. *The Richardson Dilworth Story.* Philadelphia: Mercury Books, Inc. 1962. (On Philadelphia politics.)

Morris, Richard B., ed. *Encyclopedia of American History.* New York: Harper & Row, Publishers, 1965.

———. *Great Presidential Decisions.* Greenwich, Conn.: Fawcett Publications, Inc., 1966.

° Moscow, Warren. *What Have You Done For Me Lately?* Englewood Cliffs, N.J.: Prenctice-Hall, Inc., 1967. (On New York politics.)

Myers, Gustavus. *History of the Great American Fortunes.* New York: The Modern Library, 1937.

° Neustadt, Richard E. *Presidential Power.* New York: The New American Library, 1964.

° Nichols, Roy F. *American Leviathan.* New York: Harper & Row, Publishers, 1963. (On history of U.S. politics.)

° Osborne, John. *The Nixon Watch.* New York: Liveright, 1970.

° ———. *The Second Year of the Nixon Watch.* New York: Liveright, 1971.

° Patman, Wright. *Our American Government and How It Works.* Toronto, New York, London: Bantam Books, Inc., 1968.

° Pearson, Drew, and Jack Anderson. *The Case Against Congress.* New York: Simon and Schuster, 1968.

° Peltason, Jack W., and James M. Burns, eds. *Functions and Policies of American Government.* Englewood Cliffs, N.J.: Prentice-Hall, Inc., 1958.

Pringle, Henry F. *Theodore Roosevelt.* New York: Harcourt, Brace & World, Inc., 1956.

Provence, Harry. *Lyndon B. Johnson.* New York: Fleet Publishing Corporation, 1964.

Pullen, John J. *Patriotism in America.* New York: American Heritage Press, 1971.

° Reedy, George E. *The Twilight of the Presidency.* New York and Cleveland: The World Publishing Company, 1970.

° Riegle, Donald, with Trevor Armbrister. *O Congress.* Garden City, New York: Doubleday & Company, Inc., 1972.

Rollins, Alfred B., Jr. *Woodrow Wilson and the New America.* New York: Dell Publishing Co., Inc., 1965.

Rubenstein, Richard E. *Rebels In Eden.* Boston, Toronto: Little, Brown and Company, 1970. (On American violence.)

Russell, Francis. *The Shadow of Blooming Grove.* New York, Toronto: McGraw-Hill Book Company, 1968. (On President Warren G. Harding.)

° Sandman, Peter M. *Students and the Law.* New York, London: Collier Books, 1971.

° Schwartz, Bernard. *The Reins of Power.* London: Chatto & Windus, 1964.

° Sherrill, Robert. *Gothic Politics in the Deep South.* New York: Grossman Publishers, 1968.

———. *The Accidental President.* New York: Pyramid Books, 1968. (On President Lyndon B. Johnson.)

Snyder, Louis L., and Richard B. Morris, eds. *They Saw It Happen.* Harrisburg, Pa.: The Stackpole Company, 1951. (Eyewitness reports of famous events.)

Spock, Benjamin. *Decent and Indecent.* New York: The McCall Publishing Company, 1970.

° Steffens, Lincoln. *Autobiography.* New York: Harcourt, Brace & World, Inc., 1958.

° ———. *The Shame of the Cities.* New York: Hill and Wang, 1957.

Stone, I. F. *Polemics and Prophecies: 1967–1970.* New York: Random House, 1972.

Syrett, Harold C., ed. *American Historical Documents.* New York: Barnes & Noble, Inc., 1960.

Thayer, George. *The Farther Shores of Politics.* New York: Simon and Schuster, 1968.

° Tolchin, Martin & Susan. *To the Victor.* New York: Random House, 1971. (On political patronage.)

Trials of the Resistance. New York: The New York Review, 1970.

Truman, Harry S. *1945: Year of Decisions.* New York: The New American Library, 1965.

———. *1946–1952: Years of Trial and Hope.* New York: The New American Library, 1965.

Wattenberg, Ben J., with Richard M. Scammon. *This U.S.A.* New York: Pocket Books, 1967.

° Weaver, Warren, Jr. *Both Your Houses.* New York, Washington, London: Praeger Publishers, 1972

Weigley, Russell F. *Towards an American Army.* New York and London: Columbia University Press, 1962.

° Weisbord, Marvin R. *Campaigning for President.* New York: Washington Square Press, Inc., 1966.

° Wheeler, Harvey. *Democracy in a Revolutionary Era.* Santa Barbara, California: The Center for the Study of Democratic Institutions, 1970.

° White, Leonard D. *The States and the Nation.* Baton Rouge: Louisiana State University Press, 1953.

° Wills, Garry. *Nixon Agonistes.* Boston: Houghton Mifflin Company, 1970.

Wilson, Woodrow. *Woodrow Wilson's Own Story.* Boston: Little, Brown and Company, 1952.

° Winter, Ella, and Herbert Shapiro, eds. *The World of Lincoln Steffens.* New York: Hill and Wang, 1962.

° Winter-Berger, Robert N. *The Washington Pay-Off.* New York: Dell Publishing Company, 1972.

° Ziegler, Edward. *The Vested Interests.* New York and London: The Macmillan Company, 1964.

Also consulted were publications of the American Civil Liberties Union and the Public Affairs Committee; and issues of *Business Week, The Center Magazine, Center Report, City, Civil Liberties, The Nation, Newsweek, New York Magazine, The New York Post, The New York Times, Ramparts, Variety* and *Wassaja.*

· Index

ABOUT THE AUTHOR

Jules Archer first became interested in writing for young people when his three sons were in high school, and in the years since then he has written more than forty-eight books of history and biography. Among the topics he has considered are the role of dissent in American society, the Philippines' fight for independence, and the rise of new leaders and new nations in Africa. His biographies include men as diverse as Metternich and Mao Tse-tung. In all his books, Mr. Archer's basic premise has been that if young readers are to make the intelligent judgments essential to a functioning democracy they must be given the whole truth about our society—our failures as well as our successes.

Born in New York City and educated at the College of the City of New York, Mr. Archer has been a copywriter for film companies and a war correspondent. With his wife, Eleanor, who assists him in his research, he lives in Pine Plains, New York.